THE BEST OF
PAINTED
FURNITURE

THE BEST OF PAINTED FURNITURE

Florence de Dampierre

Foreword by Peter Krueger
Design by Paul Hardy

RIZZOLI
NEW YORK

TO AYMAR

First published in the United
States of America in 1987 by
Rizzoli International Publications, Inc.,
300 Park Avenue South,
New York, NY 10010

Reprinted 1991, 2000

Library of Congress Cataloging-in-Publication Data

Dampierre, Florence de.
    The best of painted furniture.

    Bibliography: p. 197
    Includes index.
    1. Painted furniture—History. I. Title.
NK2703.D36   1987   749.2   86–43192
Paperback edition, 1995,
ISBN 0-8478-1886-1

Translated from the French by
Franklin Phillip

Set in type by David Seham
Associates Inc.
Metuchen, New Jersey

Printed and bound in Hong Kong

CONTENTS

FOREWORD

A popular misconception among the general public is that rooms decorated in the eighteenth century were blandly colorless and lacked painted decoration, polychromed walls, or painted furniture. This is quite untrue. Because eighteenth-century craftsmen favored softer, less expensive, and less durable woods for furniture that was to be painted, a good deal of it has not survived into the twentieth century. As a result, most of the furniture known from that time is either veneered or carved of solid, undecorated woods. In fact, much of the furniture produced in England and the Continent during this period was painted, and it was often extremely sophisticated.

Many designers created painted furniture to work with the specific scheme of decoration for an actual room. Architects and designers not only provided drawings for the decoration of wall surfaces, window treatments, upholstery, mirrors, and inset painted panels meant for overdoors and overmantels, but also for the actual pieces of furniture integral to the overall design. When the walls were decorated with polychromed motifs, the furniture often echoed the painted elements.

The first three quarters of the nineteenth century saw a decline in the fashion for painted furniture; the revivals of the Gothic, Renaissance, and Baroque styles precluded the use of the comparatively delicate painted furniture used by eighteenth-century architects. It was not until the last quarter of the nineteenth century that more lighthearted, whimsical, and smaller-scaled furniture again became popular. With this trend the revival of interest in painted furniture became inevitable. The early twentieth century saw such maverick interior designers as Elsie de Wolfe and Syrie Maugham beginning to incorporate pieces of painted furniture into their designs. Clearing out the clutter and darkness of late nineteenth-century interiors, they painted a variety of surfaces, washed and stenciled floors and walls, and incorporated painted furniture into their plans. Pieces of veneered furniture were pickled and decorated, thereby restoring a sense of light and finesse that had been present in the painted interiors of the late eighteenth century.

Today interest in painted furniture continues to be renewed. In this book Florence de Dampierre has captured current fascination with this style of decoration. Although contemporary designers no longer adhere to the eighteenth-century practice of coordinating the design of the room and the decoration of the furniture, de Dampierre illustrates that individual pieces of painted furniture have great relevance to modern rooms. The eighteenth century becomes in these pages an era of brilliant color and intricate pattern that can transform today's rooms into harmonious environments of elegant beauty. Her choice of eighteenth-century pieces is diverse and fascinating, ranging from grandly sophisticated French and Italian examples to the simpler, more provincial American and northern European pieces. And her selection of contemporary rooms that utilize painted pieces shows the use of painted furniture to great advantage. With a well-trained eye, an understanding and appreciation for painted furniture, and a clarity of expression, Florence de Dampierre demonstrates that painted furniture can continue to live on for centuries more.

Peter Krueger
Vice President in charge of
French and Continental
Furniture
Christie's

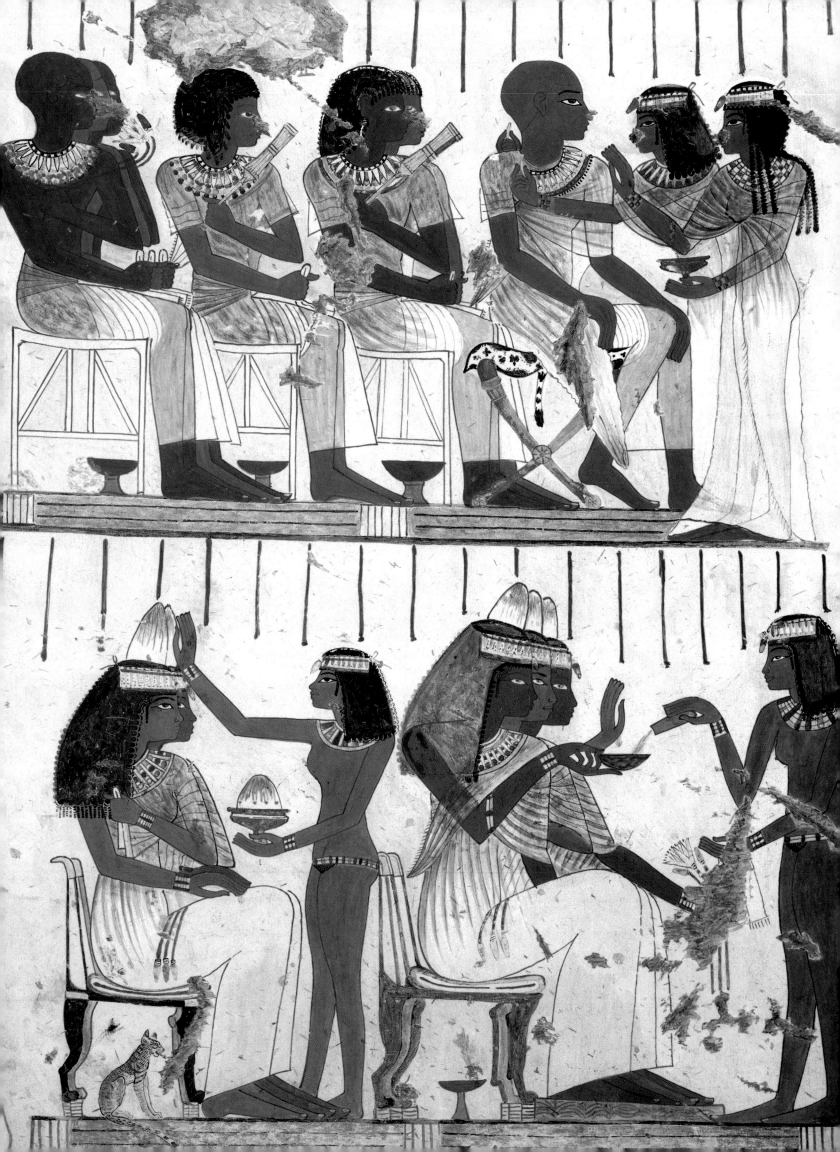

INTRODUCTION

From prehistoric times to the present day, painting has been, along with drawing, the primary form of visual expression. Wherever paint appears—on canvases, on murals and frescos, or on household objects—it brightens everyday life. Painted furniture, which combines the color and vitality of paint with the three-dimensional forms of wood and metal, is the ideal outlet for the desire to embellish and enhance our surroundings.

Painted furniture has adorned dwellings from the most humble to the most sophisticated, from royal palaces and country estates to middle-class apartments and rustic farmhouses. Its geographical range is equally wide: in the eighteenth and nineteenth centuries, when painted furniture reached its peak in western Europe, it could be found from the Atlantic coast to the steppes of Russia, from the fiords of Norway to the shores of the Mediterranean. Today the best of painted furniture is appreciated for its vibrancy, its versatility, its whimsy, and its warmth.

The evolution of painted furniture has, like the development of other aspects of civilization, fluctuated with the impulses of fashion, politics, and wealth. The ancient Egyptians perfected the art of painting on wood, as the impressive painted and gilded burial objects from their tombs bear witness. The method they used was simple but effective: they first coated their wooden coffers, chairs, and sarcophagi with a thin layer of adhesive plaster, which yielded a satin-smooth surface. To this absorbent plaster they applied their pigments, which dried quickly, imparting a brilliant sheen to the finished piece. With a few modifications, this method has been used to the present day.

Although the decorative innovations and imagery of ancient Egypt were well appreciated by Europeans, especially after the Napoleonic expeditions, it was increased contact with the Orient that inspired the European rage for paint on

A sycamore coffin from Thebes of the XVIIth–XVIIIth dynasties (about 1668–1450 B.C.) employs the paint-over-gesso technique developed by the ancient Egyptians. From the Metropolitan Museum of Art, New York

In the copy of the ancient Egyptian wall painting on the opposite page, from the collection of the Metropolitan Museum of Art, New York, a banqueting scene shows the types of painted chairs used by Egyptians about 1380 B.C.

Roman painted furniture, uncovered at the site of Pompeii in the eighteenth century, inspired artisans working in the Neoclassical style. This room from the Boscoreale is at the Metropolitan Museum of Art, New York.

The European fascination with Chinese culture led to many expressions of chinoiserie. This drawing shows the first Chinese porcelain pavilion built in France.

furniture, through the ancient art of lacquer. The precise date of the invention of lacquer is unknown, but fragments of lacquered objects have been discovered along with other burial goods in tombs of the Han dynasty (206 B.C.–A.D. 25). From then on lacquered objects from every dynasty are known in China, but apparently manufacture reached a height in about 1680, when the emperor Ķ'ang Hsi—noted for his cultivation of the arts—established a royal factory next to the imperial palace in Peking.

At its most sophisticated, ancient oriental lacquering was an extremely time-consuming and exacting art. Based on the sap of the sumac plant, *Rhus vernicifera,* the lacquer was colored with the addition of cinnabar, which produced a red liquid, and charred bone meal, which produced black. Using a fine brush, the artisan applied a thin layer of this viscous substance to a highly polished soft wood, then followed with a thicker layer laid on with a spatula. After each successive layer had dried for at least twelve hours, the surface was buffed to a high polish before the next was applied. In all, twelve to sixteen base coats were required before decoration could begin, and another three to six additional layers to finish the piece. Complicating this laborious method was a peculiar property of lacquer: it becomes hard upon exposure to air, but harder still in the presence of moisture, which naturally slows the drying interval.

Lacquer arrived in Japan from China by way of Korea, which invaded the islands in about the sixth century A.D. By the sixteenth century, the Japanese had surpassed their teachers in their mastery of the art.

European fascination with the Orient began long before the importation of oriental lacquer—when Marco Polo brought back tales of his adventures in the mysterious East in the thirteenth century. As maritime trade routes became firmly established in the seventeenth century—primarily spurred by the European quest for spices—Europeans began to develop tastes for other oriental products. The English, Dutch, and French East India companies, licensed under the charters of their kings, loaded a few precious porcelain objects—known as *objets de Chine*—onto their ships and introduced them to the courts of Europe. First mentioned in the 1524 inventory of Margaret of Austria, porcelain became an increasingly significant part of the China trade in the seventeenth, eighteenth, and nineteenth centuries.

The history of Europe's enchantment with lacquer took a somewhat different course. In 1682, Louis XIV received at Versailles the first ambassador from Siam, who brought rare and precious gifts. On behalf of the Siamese queen, the emissary presented the French queen with "a small Japanese table glazed in red" and the king with "a bedstead of the same origin." In Holland, the Dutch East India Company prompted a growing trend for lacquered furniture bedecked with flowers, fruit, and ribbons. As passion grew throughout Europe for everything from the Far East, royal patrons commissioned extravagant expressions of their affection. It soon became necessary for every court to boast a Chinese pavilion, or, failing that, at least a room fitted out with lacquer and porcelains in the Chinese style. The most exquisite representation of this taste was reputedly Madame de Pompadour's Trianon de Porcelaine at Versailles, alas no longer extant.

One of the most elaborate Chinese pavilions was built on the grounds of the Drottningholm Castle near Stockholm in the eighteenth century. Furnished with Chinese-style painted furnishings, it features a pagoda cupola.

Struggling with the difficulties of importing enough lacquered furniture to meet the seemingly insatiable appetites of royal and noble patrons, cabinetmakers ordered sets of lacquered panels from China and Japan and attached them to skeletal frames, producing armoires and commodes. The system was less than satisfactory, however, since the panels the oriental lacquerers produced often could not be adapted to European furniture designs: patterns could not be pieced together seamlessly or even with any continuity. In addition, an order for lacquer panels was not always delivered promptly. The nature of the process meant that months—even years—might be required to produce enough lacquer for the simplest cabinet, and the time needed for dispatching an order and transporting the finished work only added to the delay. Eventually, cabinetmakers and their royal sponsors sought to solve the problem by fostering domestic manufacture of the ware, an effort that met with resounding success.

The French were the first to achieve noteworthy results. In the flurry of creative activity that characterized the reign of Louis XIV (1643–1715) there emerged a special method for treating furniture, objects, and paneling. This became known as vernis Martin, after Guillaume Martin and his three brothers, who were its most skillful and famous users. By the mid-eighteenth century it seemed as if there were few wooden objects in the royal households of Europe that had not been glazed and colored by the Martins—or by other artisans whom their achievements had inspired.

The cream paint of this Italian commode suits the color scheme of a contemporary room designed by Robert Metzger for a New York apartment. Painted furniture, with its long tradition in the decorative arts, blends well with modern settings.

Elsewhere in Europe, lacquer prompted a similarly enthusiastic response. Under the influence of French taste, the principalities of Italy embraced the art, inaugurating adaptations that made the style their own. Italian lacquerers, known as *depentori,* perfected a lacquering technique, then simplified it with *lacca contrafatta*—a method that substituted colored paper reproductions for painstaking brushwork. In Britain, painted furniture gained favor during the reign of William and Mary (1689–1702). The technique of japanning, as English lacquering is known, was discovered in the seventeenth century and grew steadily in popularity. The height of English painted furniture, however, was probably in the late eighteenth and early nineteenth centuries, when the influence of the classical style, revived by such talented architects as Robert Adam, inspired delicately painted garlands of flowers and arabesques on golden satinwood backgrounds. In Prussia, Frederick II decorated his country retreat Sans Souci in vernis Martin; in Sweden the cabinetmaker's guild, which regarded itself as an offshoot of the French guild, avidly took up the French fashion; and in Denmark the king built one of the earliest chinoiserie pavilions in Europe. In 1717, while visiting the Gobelins lacquer atelier managed by Gerhard Dagly, Peter the Great was so impressed with the "Chinese-style painted and gilded pieces for the king" that he ordered similar wares to take back to Russia. Thus, lacquerware made its way across Europe in an active exchange of ideas and techniques—and even of artisans, the best of whom traveled from court to court, adorning palaces in every corner of Europe.

While these talented cabinetmakers decorated the chambers of princes, the everyday craftsmen of Europe were busy developing their own tradition of painted furniture based on the decorative ideas of the Middle Ages and Renaissance. This parallel movement was equally vibrant, and, in many cases, equally refined. Taking root particularly in the mountainous regions of Central Europe—the Tyrol, Bavaria, the Appenzell region of Switzerland, and Alsace—where long winters indoors gave ample opportunity for the development of craft, painted furniture prospered through the nineteenth century, each region giving rise to its own designs and styles. Sometimes rustic in conception, these functional pieces had great vitality. They figure prominently in the evolution of folk art in these regions, and in Scandinavia, Russia, and Poland, as well.

The painted furniture craze of the eighteenth century spread as far as Poland, where it brightened the interior of this castle with its painted walls, gilded settee, and harp.

Designer Mario Buatta demonstrates the use of painted furniture to balance color and form in the arrangement of a room. The painted chair at the left suits an eclectic combination of other furnishings.

A romantic interpretation of French nineteenth-century painted furniture is the bedroom by David Anthony Easton on the opposite page.

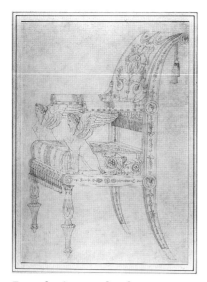

Few designers had as pervasive an influence on the decorative style of their times as the early nineteenth-century architects Charles Percier and Pierre Fontaine. Their drawing of a chair above shows the mixed influences that made up the Empire style—Egyptian, classical, and European.

Although the painted furniture tradition began to wane in the second half of the nineteenth century, it found some new proponents in the Neo-Gothic style. The English architect William Burges designed many examples of painted furniture in his career, beginning about 1858. This drawing dates to the late nineteenth century.

Mark Hampton's design for a living room shows the range of uses for paint in contemporary rooms: the painted walls are accented by gilded and painted chairs and especially by a handsome painted English longcase clock (opposite).

Whether elegant or simple, painted furniture endured in popularity into the nineteenth century because of its adaptability to new styles. As Neoclassical influences replaced the Rococo during the second half of the eighteenth century, cabinetmakers responded with delicate colors and less exaggerated lines. The opulence of the Empire style, which swept the Continent in the wake of Napoleon's army in the early nineteenth century, may have suited itself to polished mahogany and gilt ormolu ornaments, but the inspiration of Roman, Greek, and Egyptian sources—as interpreted by Napoleon's favorite architects Charles Percier and Pierre Fontaine—continued to inspire fine works with painted finishes.

Toward the middle of the nineteenth century, when the taste for painted furniture began to wane, it found a final efflorescence in the surge of popularity for papier-mâché, in France, where it first arrived in Europe (and its name was coined), in Germany, and especially in England, where it was one of the hallmarks of Victorian taste—laden with dark lacquer and inset with mother-of-pearl. Even America had its papier-mâché factories, which extended the life of this art into the late nineteenth century.

The ascendancy of painted furniture in America was as strong as its rise in Europe, but as with all New World arts, American painted furniture took on a look and interpretation of its own. Mingling such disparate influences as German Pennsylvania Dutch with that of British Chippendale, America produced results unique in the painted-furniture repertoire.

Although furniture may still be painted today, the use of paint as an essential decorative element—meant to be blended as part of a design for architectural elements, walls, and ceilings, as well as furnishings—had largely died out by the end of the nineteenth century. Even the peasant tradition lapsed, as isolated regions became incorporated into the overall culture of German-speaking countries, and folk arts fell into disuse. An occasional revival—the Omega Workshops of the British Bloomsbury school, for example—failed to reestablish the preeminence that painted furniture had enjoyed during its peak.

What is left of this grand tradition today is a record of its rise and fall, its origins in ancient sources, and its continual revival of ancient skills and ancient designs. The best of painted furniture is a treasury of the finest objects inspired by man's creative instincts.

FRANCE

During the reign of Louis XV (1715–74), the art of lacquering, introduced from the Orient in the late seventeenth century, increased in popularity, abetted by a number of changes in social as well as decorative style. The grand palace of Versailles remained the king's primary residence, but in royal palaces, Parisian townhouses, and provincial châteaux alike, the enormous reception halls and ballrooms were being supplemented or replaced with salons and intimate chambers, where visitors could be received privately. These smaller-scale rooms could not accommodate the massive furniture of the Louis XIV period and were instead fitted with diminutive, delicate pieces with soft, rounded curves and intricate ornamentation. Although reduced in size, these daintier commodes and chairs now appeared in greater quantities, and for the first time furniture was selected and placed with regard for the entire room, becoming an integral part of the setting for which it was designed.

The detail of a ceiling above and the mural on the opposite page are both from the eighteenth-century Château de Saint-Marcel-de-Félines near the Massif Central, formerly in the Chalmez family and now owned by the comtesse Laurent des Garets. The ceiling still has traces of moats and a drawbridge of a castle scene. The mural, from the Conte des Garets room, is painted with fabulous grotesques in khaki and dark ocher. At the right the semicircular commode of about 1755 from the Ferdinand de Rothschild collection, now at Waddesdon Manor, Aylesbury, has a port scene in vernis Martin lacquer and is stamped I. DUBOIS. The carcase is of oak and pine; the front legs are of sycamore.

19

With its rich colors, gilded details, and range of applications, lacquered furniture was ideal for this new vision of interior decoration, and it quickly became the rage of French society. So much attention was paid to new trends in interiors, in fact, that by the end of the eighteenth century the writer Louis Sébastien Mercier remarked in his *Tableau de Paris* (1781–90), "Furniture has become the principal object of luxury and of expenditure. One changes furnishings every six years so as to obtain everything inspired by the latest fashion."

The precise date when varnish—made from copal, a plant gum dissolved in oil—began to be manufactured in France is not known. It was apparently used before 1661, when Nicolas Foucquet, Louis XIV's superintendent of finance, recorded in the royal inventory "two red-varnished pedestal tables (European-made)." Later, in 1713, a craftsman named Gerhard Dagly obtained the necessary patent for varnishing, thereafter directing an atelier in the Gobelins factory. And another inventory of royal possessions in 1720 mentions "one table, painted and varnished in the porcelain style." The technique

In the salon of the Château de Saint-Marcel-de-Félines, the white painted chairs and settee blend with other eighteenth-century furnishings and with the walls, also painted in the eighteenth century.

21

was well enough known by 1738 to prompt learned discussions of Chinese lacquer in the June and August issues of *Mercure*. By the time of Louis XV, many craftsmen practiced the art—including François-Elie Vincent, painter and lacquerer to the king, and the celebrated Sieur Jean-Félix Watin, whose *L'Art du peintre, doreur, vernisseur* (1772) became a classic manual. But it was four brothers—Guillaume, Simon-Etienne, Julien, and Robert Martin—who were to receive the highest praise for their interpretation of lacquer art.

So famous were the Martins that their vernis Martin—a distinctive, usually green, varnish enhanced by gold dust—became synonymous with the new lacquer. In his first treatise on the inequality of human conditions, Voltaire wrote of "paneled ceilings gilded and varnished by Martin," and later he mentions "these chambers where Martin has surpassed the art of China." His comedy *Nanine* refers satirically to this new passion of the rich: "Six beaux chevaux, vous serez content/ Tous les panneaux sont de Martin vernis. . . ." The opulence that the vernis Martin represented inspired wrath in other intellectuals of the day: the political activist Mirabeau vehemently protested "the carriages varnished by Martin."

Sons of a tailor, the Martins reached this level of renown over the course of several years. Guillaume, the eldest brother, began the practice of his trade as a painter of carriages. From 1730 to 1749 he was the head lacquerer to the king. His brothers followed him in his profession: a 1744 council decree gave Simon-Etienne Martin an exclusive (needless to say, exclusive except for Guillaume) "twenty-year monopoly on the manufacture of all sorts of pieces in relief in the Japanese and Chinese style." The leaders in their field by 1745, the Martins were increasingly occupied by the ever-growing number of

Hunt scenes, like those on the bracket of the fine Louis XV vernis Martin clock at the left, were typical of painted decoration of the eighteenth century, along with other pastoral subjects. The clock is stamped FRANÇOIS DU BOIS A PARIS on the face and the backplate and carries another stamp, JME. On the bracket is the stamp DUHAMEL; François Duhamel specialized in clock cases beginning in about 1750. At the right, another room from the Château de Saint-Marcel-de-Félines. The Chalmazel Room is the only one in the château to have still lifes and landscapes painted directly on the wood paneling. A few pieces of furniture have also been touched by the painter's brush.

commissions for their varnished furnishings. In 1748 a public notice reported that "the royal factory of MM. Martin for fine Chinese varnishes is located on the faubourg Saint-Martin, the faubourg Saint-Denis, and another on the rue Saint-Magloire." The public became so infatuated with the Martins' work that the glorious ceiling by André-Charles Boulle that Louis XIV had commissioned for his son at Versailles was destroyed and replaced by a decoration on a green background executed by the Martins. Louis XV's notorious mistress Madame de Pompadour so admired the precious furnishings adorned in vernis Martin that she ordered great quantities of them for her Château de Bellevue.

French taste influenced stylistic trends throughout Europe, and it soon became de rigueur for European royalty to employ the Martins to apply their signature colors and delicate techniques to the interiors of palaces and country dwellings. The Prussian emperor, Frederick the Great, summoned Jean-Alexandre Martin, Robert's son, to decorate his palace Sans Souci (1745–47). And at the time of Guillaume Martin's death in 1749, some of his relatives were decorating the apartments of the dauphin and his dauphine at Versailles.

A decree of 15 April 1753 extolling the Martins for achieving the highest level of perfection in their art describes the processes the brothers used: "When the pieces [to be decorated] have reached the first state

The fashion for Chinese porcelain and its imitations in blue-and-white pottery affected the decoration of furniture as well. These eighteenth-century pieces have the color schemes and decorative arabesques of faience. The *encoignure*, or corner cupboard, on the opposite page is signed CRIAERD and dates to about 1743. It is in the collection of the Musée du Louvre, Paris. Above and below is an interesting table from the Blue Salon of the Musée Carnavalet, Paris, with a drawer on one side and rustic feet instead of fancy brass sabots.

The taking of snuff, introduced from the American colonies by way of England in 1556, became fashionable among French gentlemen in the eighteenth century, and with it the use of fancy snuffboxes. The oval box above is mounted in gold and decorated both top and bottom with frolicking putti on clouds. A box for storing small personal items from a woman's repertoire, such as bodkins, needles, and scissors, called an *etui*, dates to about 1760 and is also decorated with putti.

[that is, the form and consistency ready for decoration], they are polished with a file or rasp to prepare them to receive paint; then they are varnished. Colors may be applied either by combining and blending them with the varnish . . . or by applying them in sections in the manner of a checkerboard, or by applying them beneath the polished varnish, or by mixing powders and metal filings with varnish into a paste, which the painter then spreads onto the particular piece." Although green was by far the most frequently used color, there are other background colors known—blue and yellow, for example. Gold dust was incorporated into the base color in imitation of the *nashiji* (pear-skin) and *taka-makie* (raised gold lacquer) processes of Japan, which were much in vogue throughout Europe at the end of the seventeenth and beginning of the eighteenth centuries.

With this technique the Martins decorated a remarkable variety of objects: from landau and berline coaches

The berline coach, invented in about 1660 by an Italian employed by the king of Prussia, represented a major technological advance in carriages. Whip springs, used in combination with leather braces, minimized the swinging motion associated with the rigid-pillar connection of the earlier models. These lighter, more elegant coaches were ideal for painted decoration. The example below was sent from France to Rome in 1785 as a gift to the marchioness Pianetta and was later used by Cardinal Painette, a high prelate to the papal court. In the detail at the right can be seen a panel with allegorical figures bordered in flowers and fruit. The banderole below the windows features eagles and couchant lions. Museums at Stonybrook, New York

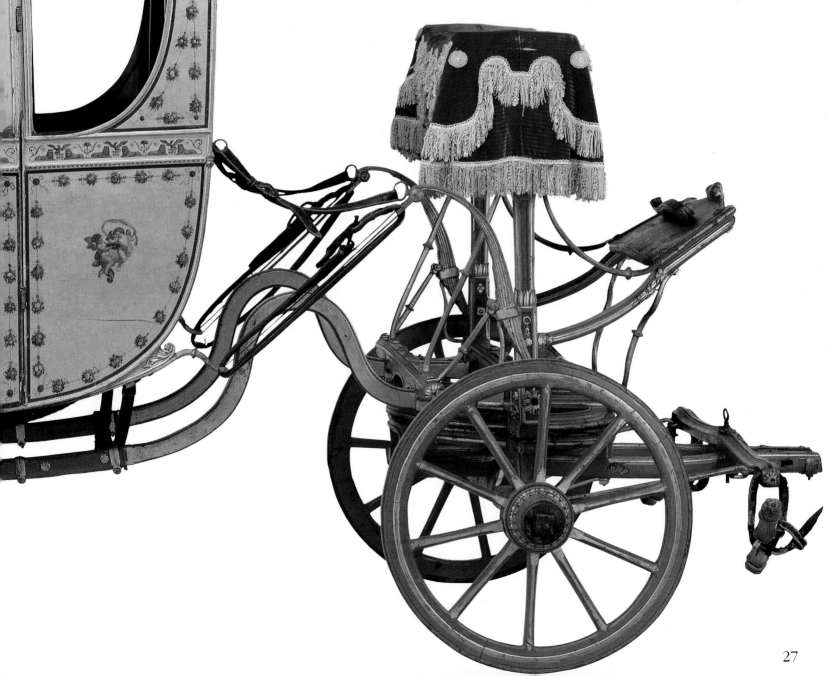

and sedan chairs to commodes, seating furniture, and smaller objects. As of 1760, the crown's household included many tables and commodes lacquered in "petit vert de Martin." Fortunately, many pieces of vernis Martin are still extant. One of the finest examples, presently in the Musée de Cluny, is the magnificent four-wheeled aventurine official carriage used by French ambassadors to Vienna under Louis XV.

After the death of Guillaume, the Martin ateliers continued to operate. Julien managed the rue Saint-Magloire atelier; Robert, who also had the title "lacquerer to the king of Prussia," directed the one on the faubourg Saint-Denis. The last workshop to remain in operation was the first to open—the faubourg Saint-Martin shop, which was carried on by Simon-Etienne. The vernis Martin technique and style was copied by other cabinetmakers, many of them achieving a similarly high level of craftsmanship. Among these was Pierre Migeon II, a protégé of Madame de Pompadour,

who showed her admiration by petitioning the king on his behalf for an annual pension of 3,000 livres, a substantial income for a craftsman at that time.

With the triumph of Neoclassicism during the reign of Louis XVI (1774–92), the Rococo excesses of the previous era fell from favor. Simple forms and plain decoration—fluting and geometrical lines—replaced the elaborate pastorals and chinoiserie of the old style. Veneering and marquetry continued to be popular, and the lacquer technique was applied to subtler treatments: trompe l'oeils in grisaille, simulating ancient

At the left and below is a light, tilt-top table with flowers, branches, birds, and in the center a coat of arms on a black background. From the yellow Louis XV Drawing Room of the Musée Carnavalet, Paris

Greek and Roman bas reliefs, and Pompeiian compositions in blue and white, in imitation of biscuitware in the style of Josiah Wedgwood.

Nearly all of the great cabinetmakers produced lacquered or, less often, painted, furniture in the Neoclassical style. Roger Vandercruse (called La Croix) who became a master craftsman in 1755, produced many pieces heavily influenced by Greek architecture; he also had a penchant for the vernis Martin style with chinoiserie. Pierre Garnier, another mid-century *maître*, produced an extraordinarily fine table in vernis Martin with a porcelain top, now in the Musée Nissim de Camondo in Paris. Several pieces of exceptional quality by Jacques Dubois, the Parisian furniture maker, are now at Waddesdon Manor in Aylesbury, England. Martin Carlin became known for his work in vernis Martin, particularly at the Château de Bellevue for Madame de Pompadour. Bernard van

The sophistication of the design and decoration of this *secrétaire à abattant* indicates that it is by a fine Parisian cabinetmaker, and the jonquil color, with its roses, flowers, and ribbons, makes it particularly rare. The drop-front desk panel of this type of *secrétaire* came into use in the Louis XV period. Musée Carnavalet, Paris

Risenburgh (known by his signature initials BVRB) was the first to use Sèvres porcelain on furniture; a table of his, in this style, is at the Musée du Louvre.

With the death of Robert Martin in 1766, the art the brothers had perfected unfortunately fell into disuse; some feeble imitations appeared in the nineteenth century, but they did not approach the earlier masterpieces in quality. Nonetheless, the nineteenth century brought forth a wealth of new techniques for painting furniture.

THE DIRECTOIRE STYLE

The fall of the monarchy in the French Revolution altered not only the course of French history, but also the course of European decorative arts. French style underwent a period of flux that was not to end until the political and cultural situation stabilized in 1804, when Napoleon crowned himself emperor. The Directoire style, so-called for the Directory that governed France from 1795 to 1799, marked a transition from the Louis XVI style to the Empire style. The classical trend already seen in the late eighteenth century now became marked by a growing interest in English design, as popularized by George Hepplewhite's *Cabinet-Maker and Upholsterer's Guide* (1788) and Thomas Sheraton's *Cabinet-Maker and Upholsterer's Drawing-Book* (1791–94). The painters of furniture were also influenced by painters of canvases—notably Jacques-Louis David, who was so affected

The beautiful chair on the opposite page, now in the Musée du Louvre, is signed by the famous cabinetmaker Jean Baptiste Tilliard (1685–1766), who made many pieces for the prince de Soubise as well as for the king and queen at Versailles. The upholstery of the seat and back are typical of the period.

The writing table above, known as a *bureau plat*, has been popular in France from the seventeenth century to the present day. The Louis XVI example above has its drawers and legs painted with swags and garlands; the top is painted in *faux marbre*.

The panels of this fine Louis XVI cylinder-front desk are painted in imitation of Chinese lacquer in the *tôle peinte* technique with Chinese figures and a stork in flight. It is stamped c.c. SAUNIER JME.

The *secrétaire à abattant* at the left and right dates from the late eighteenth century and is in the Louis XVI style. Its fine decoration includes garlands of flowers and baskets of fruits, as well as fancy ormolu mounts.

by the classical revival that he had Roman-style chairs produced for his atelier by Georges Jacob, a leading furniture manufacturer, and Hubert Robert, a Neoclassical painter known for his architectural subjects.

Between 1785 and 1790, several architects and decorators—among them Jean-Jacques Le Queu, Aubert Parent, and Jean-Démosthène Dugourc—produced designs for exteriors, interiors, and furnishings that were to determine the direction of both the Directoire and Empire styles. These designs were directly inspired by models from antiquity—for example, Dugourc's 1780 design for the Coupole de la Bagatelle.

In keeping with the eighteenth-century interpretation of the classical style, Directoire furniture was always painted, usually in white and gold, and its ornamentation was characterized by understatement and a severity of line. Most of the Directoire style pieces that were ultimately produced were chairs, none of large proportions.

THE EMPIRE STYLE

Two architects, Charles Percier and Pierre Fontaine, reigned without peer over French decorative arts for the first fifteen years of the nineteenth century. Percier found in classical mythology the inspiration for a parade of gods, heroes, and nymphs; Fontaine strove to recreate antiquity itself. "It is a delusion to imagine that there are shapes better than those the ancients have handed down to us. We endeavor to imitate the spirit, principles, and wisdom of antiquity," they wrote in the preface to the 1812 edition of their *Recueil des décorations intérieures*. More than ever before, interior decoration was the exclusive province of a single individual: the architect. He designed

An important—and impos-
ing—Neoclassical commode
with vernis Martin on polished wood and elaborate
ormolu mounts. Attributed
to Etienne-Louis Boullée it is
stamped JOSEPH three times
and dates to about 1770.

not only the building structure but also the ceilings, draperies, furniture, and decorative objects inside it. More than the other architects of their day, Percier and Fontaine achieved a conceptual unity of design. As they explained in the *Recueil,* "Furnishings are too closely tied to interior decoration for the architect to be indifferent to them."

In the Empire period, mahogany and beechwood were the woods most often used for furniture. Beechwood pieces were gilded, silvered, or painted—like the Directoire chairs—in white and gold, and were most often found in the imperial residences. Ordinary articles of furniture for

Harps figured prominently in proper drawing-room decor of the late eighteenth century, and quite a few examples have survived. The one shown in the detail at the left has a pastoral scene of a rustic hut in the woods. Musée Carnavalet, Paris

Following pages: The pomp of Napoleon I's reign extended even to the decoration of his bathroom at the Château de Rambouillet. A relatively modest tin tub is surrounded by painted and gilded walls with Empire motifs—swans, griffins, and Mercury figures bearing laurel branches.

A rustic scene above is a detail of the foot of the eighteenth-century harp below. The leafy gilded mounts are typical of this age of curlicues and flourishes. Musée Carnavalet, Paris

A drawing by Pierre Ransom done in Paris in about 1770, and now in the Cooper-Hewitt Museum in New York, shows an elaborately painted room with a daybed in a niche. The room on the opposite page gives another example of painting used in a room setting: the collection of porcelain and glass in the Chalmazel Room of the Château de Saint-Marcel-de-Félines rests on shelves painted in the eighteenth century beneath an interesting ceiling border with medallions.

everyday use were made of mahogany of lesser quality, often painted plain white or gray. The shapes of the Empire style were even more severe than those of the Directoire, and were heavier in proportion, but this appropriately imperial weightiness was softened by a varied repertoire of decorative ornaments. Palm-leaf moldings were favored, but laurel, oak, and ivy leaves—often arranged in crowns—also appeared. The most widely used motifs were Napoleonic symbols—the bee, along with the eagle, the swan, and the lyre. Just as the reign of Napoleon was never to be equaled in French history, the domination of Percier and Fontaine was never challenged. After

To make their country homes look inhabited when they were away, eighteenth-century aristocrats used painted figures called dummy boards. These unusual ecclesiastical figures engrossed in conversation—no doubt intended to impress passersby with the piety of the owners—come from the Château de Saint-Cloud.

42

The blue lacquered *secrétaire en dos d'âne*—a writing desk with two sides so that two people may sit facing each other—was made for Madame de Pompadour for her Château de Bellevue. Musée des Arts Décoratifs, Paris

the Empire style, the influence of France in furniture fashions, along with the fortunes of France itself, was to decline.

THE RESTAURATION STYLE

The Restauration style, ushered in with the Bourbon king Louis XVIII in 1814, marked the end of the long reign of Neoclassicism. Furniture retained the massive lines of the Empire style, but mahogany was used infrequently, as light-colored woods came into fashion. Painted furniture was nearly nonexistent.

For a few years during the reign of Louis-Philippe (1830–48), and again during the Second Empire (1852–70), lacquered furniture enjoyed a revival. Now manufactured for middle-class clients—certainly a novelty in furniture trends—the new lacquered furniture achieved great popularity. Generally made of ebonized pearwood, lacquered in black, and adorned with multicolored painted flowers, the finer examples were also

A marble-topped commode decorated in the manner of Pierre Ransom. Black lacquer was the most frequently used background color for chinoiserie designs.

A stag scene on the front of the commode at the right and scenes from La Fontaine's fables are in polychrome lacquer adapted from a design by Jean Baptiste Oudry. The bombé style of the chest itself is transitional, probably of about 1760. Below the marble, on the left front corner, is the stamp J.A. GRANDJEAN.

Following pages: Empress Josephine's drawing room at Château de Malmaison preserves this pair of chairs, designed in the gondola style by Jacob-Desmalter (who worked from 1803 to 1825) around 1804. Spectacularly gilded, they feature arms fashioned as swans, one of the symbols of Napoleon.

A tilt-top *guéridon*, a candlestand, with a circular top showing a classical lyre with fruit and flowers.

One of a pair of Charles X parcel-gilt and simulated porphyry jardinières of the early nineteenth century.

embellished with copper, ivory, and mother-of-pearl inlays. Some chairs were made of papier-mâché rather than wood, a method also practiced in England at this time. These lightweight, easily moved seating elements—so unlike their ponderous predecessors—had backs in a variety of forms. There also appeared footstools and wooden chairs sculpted and painted to resemble rope. To furnish conservatories and winter gardens, now becoming fashionable, delicate chairs were designed in rattan, sometimes to simulate bamboo and usually painted.

At the Exposition Universelle in Paris in 1867, new techniques of painting furniture were offered, and at the turn of the century the designer Louis Majorelle introduced his furniture in the Japanese and Chinese style. Despite the innovations, the golden age of painted furniture in France was drawing to a close. Certain craftsmen—the bronzesmith and cabinetmaker Henri Dasson, for example—revived eighteenth-century techniques, including vernis Martin. But these revival pieces lacked the grace, elegance, and delicacy of the works that inspired them.

A nineteenth-century table with a design of birds and leaves presages the Art Nouveau style.

A small table of the eighteenth century in vernis Martin in imitation of marquetry, with a decorated porcelain top. Signed BVRB. Musée du Louvre, Paris

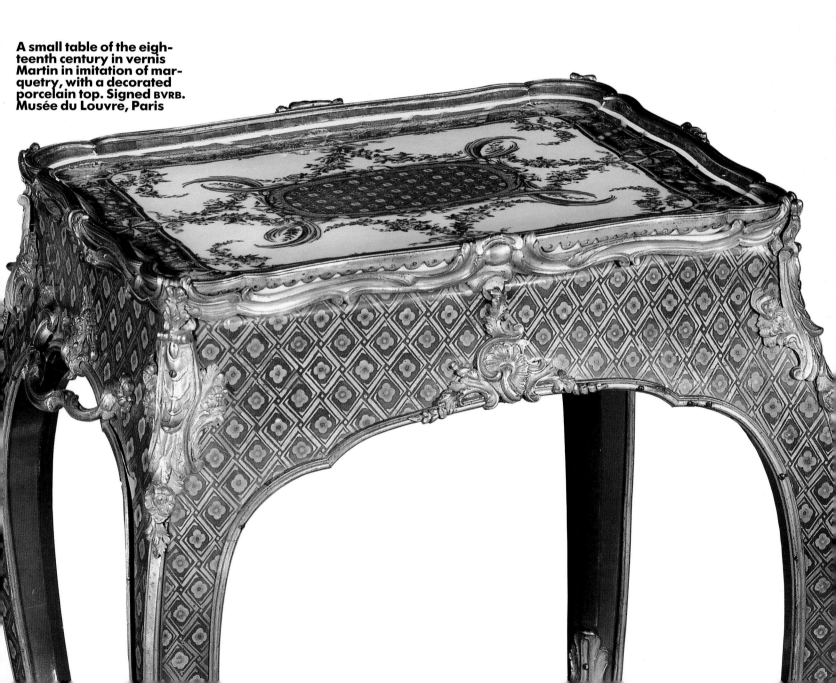

I T A L Y
S P A I N   A N D   P O R T U G A L

A loose federation of many small kingdoms and states at the beginning of the eighteenth century, Italy was politically unstable and
therefore vulnerable to the ambitions of other European powers.
Genoa was cut off from the greater part of her territories; Austria
had annexed Milan and Mantua. With the death of the last of the
Farnese princes, a Bourbon prince now governed Parma, and the
strict house of Hapsburg-Lorraine ruled Florence. Thus, the only
fully independent states of any importance in Italy were the
Republic of Venice and the papacy in Rome. Despite the low fortunes of the Venetian state, Venetian society was gay and extensive
(the old nobility included more than 450 families, of whom 200
were wealthy or very wealthy). The Venetians, with their traditional
love of festivals and elegance, were perhaps the first Italians to abandon the heavy,
ostentatious Spanish taste in favor of the frivolous Parisian model. Soon all of Italy
had once again come under the influence of France and adopted the language
and fashions of the French court, often outdoing the French themselves.

Italian painted furniture is
typically heavier in its lines
and more emphatic in its
decoration than its French
counterpart. The grotesque
mask painted on canvas (inset above) is a detail from a
pair of shutters from the end
of the eighteenth century.
Grotesque imagery derived
from ancient Roman models
was first revived in the Renaissance and again became
popular throughout Europe
in the Baroque and Rococo
styles. The Rococo Venetian
bench (*panchetta*) at the left,
painted yellow with gilded
and polychrome details, was
originally made for the
Palazzo Donà dalle Rose in
Venice in the eighteenth
century. Caramoor House
Museum, Katonah. On the
opposite page is another
Venetian piece—a chest of
drawers with *lacca contrafatta* cutouts and ormolu
mounts.

The eighteenth century in Italy was as superficial and lighthearted as the seventeenth century had been somber and introspective. Venice, city of carnivals, became the center of attraction for high-living Europeans. So illustrious was its company that when Voltaire's Candide dines in Venice with six foreigners, each is revealed to be a king. In this atmosphere of perpetual festival, two o'clock in the morning was the most appropriate and elegant hour for conversation and every hour of the day found the affluent members of Venetian society emptying their pockets and bank accounts in order to display their wealth and maintain appearances.

The tone of Venetian society, and consequently of Venetian decoration, was livelier and less formal than that at Versailles. The fashion for small apartments with intimate salons, which

This extravagant sofa, called a *canapè a ventaglio*, is probably of poplar, painted blue and gilded. It is upholstered *à chassis*—on the back and arms—in a needlework design of fruit, flowers, and foliage. Caramoor House Museum, Katonah, New York. Similar *canapè* are featured in the *Ville dei Setoli XVII e XVIII in Piemonte* by Augusto Pedrini and are apparently typical of Piedmont furniture of the eighteenth century. Below, a chinoiserie box on stand.

The *lacca contrafatta* technique, though developed to make it possible for cabinet-makers to produce complicated designs without hiring a painter, could yield lavish and impressive results. This secretary is an excellent example of Venetian work of about 1720 to 1730. Among the array of scenes on panels and drawers is the hunt on horseback shown on the opposite page. The Metropolitan Museum of Art, New York

distinguished Louis XV society from the court of his predecessor, quickly won approval in Venice. (The Ca' Rezzonico contains a fine example of this kind of room.) This development permitted the creation of interiors of incomparable charm, decorated with painted ceilings, painted paneling, and, of course, painted furniture.

The *depentori*, the first craftsmen in Italy to imitate the widely admired oriental lacquers, began to ply their trade early in the eighteenth century. At first the Venetians, in their usual spirit of levity, failed to achieve the durable quality of lacquer mastered by the French craftsmen, producing only a coarse surface. Concerned about the inferiority of their technique, the Italians produced several essays on the proper method for duplicating Chinese lacquers, notably the *Trattato sopra la vernice commune-mente detta cinese* written by Filippo Bonanni in 1720; a second edition appeared in 1731 and a French translation in 1733. The treatise offers a step-by-step description of the Chinese process and instructions for refining the finish by dissolving the varnish base in alcohol or boiled linseed oil.

An eighteenth-century writer called Morazzoni, however, offered the best description of the Italian method: First the wood was sanded smooth and coated with gesso, a mixture of glue diluted in plaster of

This chair is from a well-preserved set of eight chairs of about 1740 with painted arabesques on the legs and a coat of arms on the back splat, all highlighted with gilding.

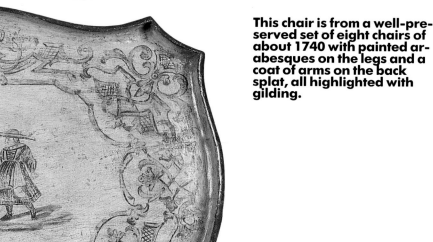

At the left, peasant figures dance delicately across a Venetian serpentine tray of the eighteenth century. The room at the right, designed by Ronald Bricke Associates, focuses on a handsome painted Italian console table of the late eighteenth century.

A side chair with the curving cabriole legs of the Rococo style, probably made in Genoa about 1735–40.

Paris, so that the joints of the piece were completely concealed. When this surface was dry it was buffed with fine sandpaper. The most skillful and conscientious artisans, following the oriental technique, next glued sheets of fine linen tightly to the surfaces to be lacquered, which accommodated any warping of the wood grain caused by changes in humidity. Having thus prepared the foundation, the *depentore* began to apply the decoration. First, he laid down the background color, then painted the desired subject in tempera. The image was often outlined in black or a dark color, using a goosefeather. Once the paint had completely dried,

The cartouche at the top of the cornice of this important Venetian *lacca contrafatta* secretary (right) suggests that it was made for a pope of the eighteenth century. It later belonged to the Grimaldi family. The four gilded wood figures surmounting the chest represent the four seasons.

The exquisite pieces on the following pages, part of a rare complete set of Venetian lacquered poplar furniture with gilding and polychrome details, belonged first to the Giovanelli family, who owned at least four palaces in Venice in the mid-eighteenth century, among them the Palazzo Donà Giovanelli. They are now in the Caramoor House Museum, Katonah, New York. A similar desk in the Ca' Rezzonico was used by a pharmacist. The armchairs are typical of Venetian style.

it was protected with several coats of sandarac varnish.

For decorations in relief, the *depentore* used a similar process. According to Morazzoni, the artisan followed the outline of the design, letting "drops of plaster and glue flow from his brush so that they were evenly distributed, each layer was equal, and above all the contours were well modulated." The paste, though liquid, had viscosity, but it was forbidden for the artist to use a stick to make corrections. In this way he obtained a kind of bas-relief just a few millimeters thick, which he then painted. Once again the *depentore* heightened the relief with outlining from a goosefeather brush, and finished the work with a few coats of varnish. Every *depentore* had a variation on this general technique—carefully guarded secret methods gleaned from his own experience.

Italian lacquered furniture appeared in a multitude of colors: cream was especially favored for backgrounds, but there were designs in coral

Carved from a close-grained reddish softwood, this tray table was first covered with a thin layer of gesso before being painted with a boating party scene on a lake beside a landscaped garden in the English taste. The tray comes from the Palazzo Reale in Turin and dates to about 1780. Caramoor House Museum, Katonah, New York

Garlands of ribbon-tied flowers are the charming decoration of this painted and gilded commode with a top in *faux marbre*. Made in Venice in the eighteenth century, it is now in the J. Paul Getty Museum, Malibu.

On the opposite page: A Venetian dressing table at Caramoor with a collection of Venetian lacquered boxes. Below: Since the carved and gilded detail of this Piedmontese armchair of about 1780 is confined to the front, the chair was probably part of a set meant to stand around the edges of a room, knee to knee, a typical arrangement throughout eighteenth-century Europe. The chairs were made for Esprit-Benôit Nicolis, conte de Robilant (1724–1801), an engineer, chemist, and mineralogist in Turin.

and scarlet, dark olive and delicate pale green, pale yellow and ivory, sky blue, pink, and pale mauve. The exciting range of applications became so admired that lacquer was soon applied to nearly every kind of household object: folding screens, spinets, armoires, as well as tiny boxes for pills, powder, cosmetics, or beauty patches. The growing demand fostered a need for a faster and less expensive process, and the *depentore* responded with *lacca contrafatta*—the use of colored cut-outs—engraved or printed designs that were glued to pieces of furniture already painted in a background color. After many coats of sandarac or plain varnish, this decoration appeared to have been painted. The prints reproduced the landscapes and genre scenes of such painters as Marco Ricci and Francesco Zuccarelli. Furniture decorated in this manner became fashionable almost instantly, and orders flowed into Venice from all over Italy. The technique was most often used to adorn large pieces, such as armoires and the large pier glasses that served as centerpieces in bedchambers and sitting rooms.

The lacquered furniture made in Venice from 1720 to 1740 featured fanciful shapes and elaborate designs in vivid colors. The most common background colors were green and black, with an occasional use of yellow and a rare, but dramatic, use of red. The shapes chosen by Venetian cabinetmakers showed the English and Dutch influences blended with the French. Among the most successful examples from this period are chests of drawers, many with tops painted in *faux marbre*. These pieces became popular outside of Venice, especially in Genoa and Turin.

The transitional period from 1760 to 1775 saw the flowering of a brilliant era in Venetian furniture. A few copies of Thomas Chippendale's *Gentleman and Cabinet-Maker's Director,* first published in 1754, made their way to Italy and further established English dominance in furniture design. Many painted Venetian pieces from this period have details borrowed from Georgian cabinetry.

Much of Venetian painted furniture was made for seaside villas and reflects the lightness of the holiday spirit. At Brescia, for example, the most popular summer retreat for Venetian society, the walls, ceilings, and even the linen or cotton hangings and draperies were painted, most frequently with charming floral motifs. Painted furniture, usually of walnut, was sparingly gilded or bronzed, and few ornaments were executed in relief. Most commodes were finished with a grand marble or *faux marbre* top. By the late eighteenth century, Modena, Parma, Piacenza, and Cremona also manufactured furniture in this style, but Venice remained the undisputed queen.

This Venetian Rococo commode dates to the mid-eighteenth century. The floral garlands are cut-outs; the green edging is painted on the yellow background.

Most Chinese decoration was painted on dark background colors; thus the dark green of this bombé commode in the Venetian Rococo style of the eighteenth century is almost black to set off the gilded landscapes and birds of the design japanned on its surface. The molded serpentine top is of *verde antico* marble.

ROME AND NEOCLASSICISM

In the second half of the eighteenth century, Neoclassicism became as fashionable in Italy as it was in England and France. Prompted by a number of well-publicized archaeological discoveries, first Herculaneum and then Pompeii, Europeans developed an insatiable appetite for the antique. Further excavations of the ruins of Hadrian's villa at Tivoli were soon followed by the discovery of Paestum. In 1755 Johann Joachim Winckelmann, the foremost archaeologist of his day, left Germany and settled in Rome to pursue his studies of Greek and Roman culture. His discoveries and book of drawings of 1759 stimulated enthusiasm for this growing science internationally, making Rome the archaeological capital of the world.

Also contributing to the development of decorating trends in Rome was the lively interchange of ideas and influences that took place between Rome and London in the last half of the eighteenth century. Lured to Rome by its rich classical resources, the Scottish architects Robert and James Adam frequently sojourned in Italy. They not only appreciated the ancient cultural artifacts, but also spread their own version of Neoclassicism in England upon their return. Likewise, a large number of Italian painters lived in London—among them Giovanni Battista Cipriani, Michaelangelo Pergolesi, and

Michaelangelo Pergolesi worked for Robert Adam in England beginning in about 1770 and many of his designs reflect Adam's influence. This exotic-looking side chair in carved and polychromed wood was made after a Pergolesi design in the late eighteenth century. The intertwined dragons and pagoda roof give it a Chinese flavor. The room at the right, by Ronald Bricke Associates, features a pair of Pergolesi chairs.

Antonio Zucchi—and they carried their own ideas back to Italy, thus closing the circle.

The key figure in Italian Neoclassical revival in Italy, as well as in France and Austria, was Giovanni Battista Piranesi. Born in Venice in 1720, Piranesi studied in Rome from 1740 to 1744 and later settled there. When his masterpiece *L'Antichità romane,* a series of etchings of Roman ruins, began to appear in 1756, it brought the theories and fragments of ancient Rome to life, and Piranesi's reputation spread throughout Europe. Acquainted with Robert Adam, Piranesi contributed several drawings to a volume of Robert and James Adam's work. For furniture trends, however, Piranesi's most influential book was *Diverse maniere d'adornare i cammini ed ogni altra parte degli edifici*, published in 1769.

The second phase of Neoclassicism, the twenty years from 1770 to 1790, marked an unprecedented era of peace in the Italian peninsula, indeed in all of Europe. In addition to Venice

The drawing above is a page from Agostino Fantastici's notebook, now in the collection of the city library of Siena. An interpretation of Neoclassical design is at the left: a Florentine table with a country scene painted on its top.

The pedestal cabinet at the left was made after a design by the prominent Sienese architect Agostino Fantastici, who was commissioned by Luigi Malavolti to design his palazzo and its furnishings about 1785. The white-and-gilt combination is typical of Neoclassic design.

and Rome, Milan became an important center for architecture and design at the end of the eighteenth century because of its Accademia di Belle Arti (founded in 1755) and the influence of one of its directors, Giocondo Albertolli, a master of the Neoclassical style. Naples also experienced an artistic flowering. In general, this held true throughout Europe, and contributed to the high level of production and quality in these two decades.

The Italians may have yielded to the French influence by this date, but they did so in an independent manner. In subject matter, Italians found suitable for including in their repertoire only a few of the motifs—flowers, angels, and ribbons—so crucial to the Louis XVI style. And, in addition, a great number of Pompeiian, Etruscan, and Roman motifs appeared in Italian painting, as did the fanciful echoes of antiquity popularized by Piranesi. The lines of pieces so decorated

Another fine piece from Wychwood, an Italian commode dating to the end of the eighteenth century, with portrait medallions on two drawers. The officer is an English dummy board of the nineteenth century, a form of painted decoration seen in Italian, French, and English homes.

Opposite page: The yellow-painted Italian desk with classical figures on a red panel is in the living room of Wychwood, J. Allan Murphy's Long Island home. At the right is one of a pair of Rococo painted and caned side chairs of about 1750.

were square and rectilinear, embellished here and there with columns, cornices and pilasters. Colors tended to follow this subdued trend—pale green, light blue, pale yellow, and myriad shades of ivory highlighted in gilt were the most frequently used.

The Neoclassical taste affected interior as well as exterior architecture. The rooms of palaces were round or oval with niches and columns; floors were frequently marble mosaic. An important innovation in interiors was the creation of the boudoir, which revolutionized bedchamber furnishings. The grand baldachins that once hovered over stately bedsteads gave way to smaller beds without canopies. With the last quarter of the eighteenth century, the use of painted furniture became firmly established. In Venice and Rome, entire bedrooms, including draperies and walls, were painted to match the ensemble of furniture, which might include a great chest of drawers, two smaller chests, an armoire, a table, a few chairs, and the bed itself.

Among the fanciful Neoclassical figures on the panels of this late eighteenth-century armoire are myriad Cupids, some framed in black medallions. The curling tendrils and swirling forms are typical of a Florentine school of decoration influenced by the Renaissance painters Giorgio Vasari and Bernardino Poccetti.

Putti frolic on this Neapolitan sedan chair carved from poplar and lindenwood, painted and gilded, and fitted with ormolu mounts around 1760. The ebullient excesses of Rococo cover nearly every surface of the chair—even the brackets through which handles slid for carrying the noble owner through the streets of Naples. The Metropolitan Museum of Art, New York

designs were soon copied by other architects and cabinetmakers, and the motifs he made popular were widely imitated. Angelica Kauffmann's work found particular favor with the public, and became widely available thanks to new methods of engraving. Many pieces of furniture were decorated with medallions taken from her pictures, most painted after she left England in 1781. Even artists as well known as William Hamilton painted furniture. A handsome Hamilton medallion appears on a cabinet designed by Sir William Chambers and constructed in 1793 by the cabinetmaking firm of Seddon and Shackleton for Charles IV of Spain.

The greatest English cabinetmakers also designed and produced painted furniture in the second half of the eighteenth century. Thomas Chippendale, whose predilection for chinoiserie resulted in the bamboolike style known as Chinese Chippendale, embraced the fashion for japanned furniture. In his illustrated trade catalogue *Gentleman and Cabinet-Maker's Director* (1754), Chippendale designates which of his furniture designs are appropriate for painting. Another notable cabinetmaker, George Hepplewhite, included in his *Cabinet-Maker and Upholsterer's Guide* (1788) many

Shown on the opposite page is a detail of the chair above. One of a pair of chairs decorated in the style of Angelica Kauffmann, the chair has a round caned-back panel painted with putti above a shaped caned seat.

The authenticity of the dressing table has inspired much debate among scholars. Chippendale designed a dressing table in which a pivoted glass was supported between two cabinets; Hepplewhite shows no dressing tables of this kind; and Sheraton illustrates a more com-plicated example in his *Drawing-Book*. Although it has been in the Victoria and Albert Museum in London since 1866, it is now considered an inspired fake of about 1862—65. The exquisite detailing of the grisaille medallions, brass moldings, and engraved silver handles nevertheless shows the maker's respect for the eighteenth-century cabinet-maker's art.

A nineteenth-century porcelain cabinet and chair in the collection of Geoffrey Shakerley. The English loved to paint putti; the caned-back armchair is another example of this affection.

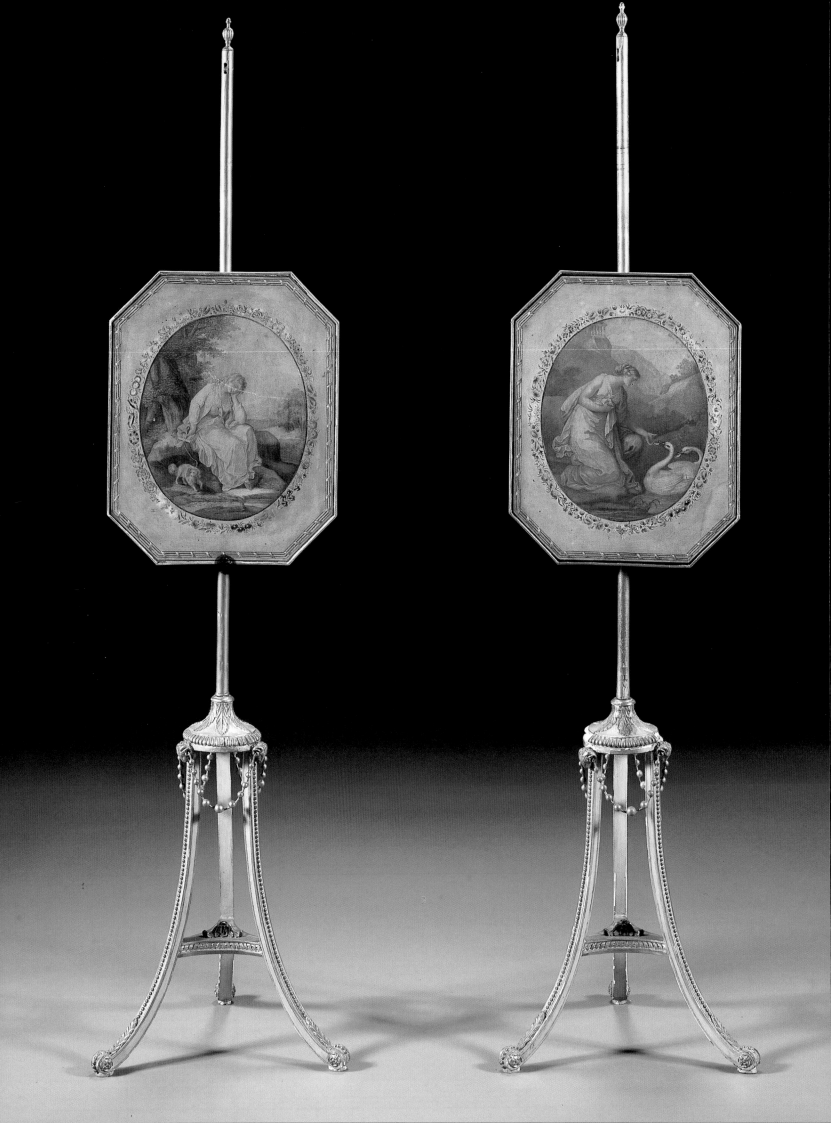

drawings of furniture pieces that appear to be painted: "the new and very elegant fashion .. arisen within these few years of finishing chairs with painted or japanned work, which gives a rich and splendid appearance to the minuter parts of the ornaments, which are so generally thrown in by the painter." He adds that "japanned chairs should have cane bottoms, with linen or cotton cases over cushions to accord with the general hue of the chair." Thomas Sheraton became famous when his *Cabinet-Maker and Upholsterer's Drawing-Book* appeared between 1791 and 1794.

Neither Hepplewhite nor Sheraton seems to have made a distinction between painted furniture and japanned furniture. Sheraton, in his *Cabinet Dictionary* (1803), refers to japanning as "a kind of painting." He also states that the colors used be the same as for a good oil painting and suggests white, Prussian blue, vermilion, and gray-green. His *Drawing-Book* discusses painting of every kind. Others, however, did make a distinction between the two techniques. Dossie's *Handmaid to the Arts* describes a technique in which colors were often applied with a water-based glue instead of varnish, and laid down directly onto the wood without a preliminary base coat.

This variation may explain why some cabinetmakers charged higher prices for japanned work than for ordinary painting. Chippendale, for example, billed Sir Edward Krachtbull for several "japanned" pieces, but in 1767 sent him an invoice listing "two large gerandoles [girandoles, a kind of candle sconce] painted blue and white."

In addition to these celebrities of cabinet design there were established cabinet-making firms, which produced painted furniture of all kinds, sometimes for these designers, sometimes from stock designs commissioned from lesser artists. Among these was George Seddon, universally regarded as the finest cabinetmaker in London in his day, with a large, highly trained staff: some eighty employees worked for the firm at the time his factory burned down in 1768. Examples of painted furniture attributed to Seddon can be seen in

The *bonheur du jour* (below) is a writing desk in typical Regency style of the late eighteenth century. Ebonized and parcel-gilt, it has a tambour slide covering a multitude of pigeonhole compartments.

To preserve a lady's delicate complexion and cultivated pallor, firescreens, such as these examples, a George III cream-painted and parcel-gilt pair of about 1770, would have shielded her from the heat, raised or lowered to the proper height. They are part of a suite of furniture made for Upton House, built around 1731 and since demolished.

The side tables on these two pages show Robert Adam's pervasive influence on the decorative arts of about 1770. In the room at the left, a bedroom from the Cara-moor House Museum in Ka-tonah, New York, the Adam-style table at the foot of the bed blends well with the Italian bedstead and French wallpaper.

A side table designed by Robert Adam for the Etruscan Room of Osterley Park, about 1775–79 (below).

many museums today, among them the satinwood armchair in the Victoria and Albert Museum in London. Another great English firm was Gillow's, which was, like Seddon's, a large family business. It was founded by Robert Gillow in Lancaster about 1728. His son Richard joined the firm around 1757, soon followed by his brothers Robert and Thomas, all of whom made painted furniture.

Both of these firms specialized in furniture of satinwood, considered by English cabinetmakers (although not by their counterparts on the Continent) to be the best-quality material for furniture. They did not paint the entire surface of this light-colored wood, but left the

area around the medallion in a natural color which they then varnished and polished. When they used beechwood, which they considered inferior, they japanned or painted it completely.

As in France and Italy, the development of Neoclassicism in England fell into two phases: the first began with Robert Adam and his followers; the succeeding, more precise and severe phase is represented by Thomas Hope. Unlike Adam, Hope was not a professional architect, but a gentleman and

Above is one of a pair of gilt wood side tables with copper top and frieze decorated in the manner of Robert Adam, about 1770.

The designer Sandra Nunnerley planned a room around this nineteenth-century mirror in an English carved and gilded frame painted with two lions rampant, badges, crests, and a playful border with foxtails. The piece bears two inscriptions, "Henricus IV Rex Anglia" and "Honi soit qui mal y pense," the motto of the Order of the Garter. At the right is one of a pair of green-painted and gilt open armchairs. Latticing and railing of splats is typical of the Sheraton style.

dilettante who wanted to create a harmonious environment for his collection of ancient sculpture, vases, and old master paintings. Born in Amsterdam to a prominent Dutch banking family, Hope traveled extensively in Europe and the Middle East from the age of eighteen. The French invasion of Holland in 1795 led him to take up residence in England, where he patronized designers and artists, commissioning them to create interiors to his taste and designs. Hope's *Household Furniture and Interior Decoration* (1807) championed classicism, especially the arts of the Greeks, and his decorations also show the influence of the Empire style of Percier and Fontaine.

This second phase of Neoclassicism bears the influence of an eclectic variety of sources, and the admiration for painted furniture nearly eliminated other forms of furniture, such as marquetry. Although England did not embrace Egyptian motifs for the same reasons as the French, Admiral Nelson's defeat of Napoleon's fleet at Abukir in 1798 inspired a taste for things Egyptian, and several extraordinary examples of furniture sporting crocodile feet bear painted scenes. (Napoleon was victorious at Abukir a year later, and his fascination with Egyptian culture made similar motifs a feature of the Empire style.)

Wychwood, the home of J. Allan Murphy on Long Island, is rich in fine English painted furniture. In this room a black lacquered Regency chair with a hand-painted flower medallion vies for attention with an early English dummy board of about 1760 and a dark green console of Adam design with an embellishment of garlands outlined in black. The Chinese coffee table in the foreground is a modern accent.

PAINTED FURNITURE IN THE NINETEENTH CENTURY

The prince regent (who became George IV at his father's death in 1820), for whom the Regency style is named, was another royal promoter of Chinese style in decoration. His fabulous Royal Pavilion (1815–22) at Brighton was filled with chinoiserie treasures, including painted furniture in exotic forms and colors. At the same time, chairs painted and sculpted to resemble bamboo began to appear, and a few years later, in the Victorian era, furniture was manufactured in papier mâché, often inlaid with mother-of-pearl, in an infinite variety of designs and shapes.

The English, perhaps more than other Europeans, were compelled during the nineteenth century to seek moral and psychological justification for their preferences in decor. This propensity characterizes two further phases—the Gothic revival period, which returned to the upward soaring forms of medieval architecture and the ecclesiastical solidity of medieval furniture; and the Arts and Crafts

The delicacy of this late eighteenth-century satinwood occasional table, painted with putti and ribbons, suits the quiet mood of this bedroom designed by Bebe Winkler Interior Design for a Park Avenue apartment in New York.

movement, which celebrated fine craftsmanship and the need for beauty in everyday life. Painted furniture found its place in both of these styles.

Toward the end of the nineteenth century, several major designers created interesting examples of painted furniture, among them the architect William Burges and the Pre-Raphaelite painters Edward Burne-Jones, who designed an unusual cabinet with painting on leather that is now in the Metropolitan Museum of Art in New York, and Dante Gabriel Rossetti, who designed a sitting room with painted furniture in the Sheraton style.

Falling again to the ephemeral whims of fashion, the vogue for painted furniture once more declined in about 1890. It was not until 1913, when the painter and art critic Roger Fry founded the Omega Workshops with fellow artists of the Bloomsbury Group— Vanessa Bell and Duncan Grant among them—that the art of painting furniture was practiced by serious designers once again. Choosing as their aesthetic principle the notion that the decorative arts should be founded upon the fine arts, the Omega Workshops produced pottery and fabrics as well as numerous pieces of painted furniture, before closing in 1920.

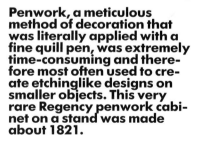

Penwork, a meticulous method of decoration that was literally applied with a fine quill pen, was extremely time-consuming and therefore most often used to create etchinglike designs on smaller objects. This very rare Regency penwork cabinet on a stand was made about 1821.

This type of washstand, which has a double folding top that protects the wall from splashes when it is raised, is illustrated by Thomas Sheraton in his *Drawing-Book* (1791), where it is described as a "Corner Bason Stand," and a stand of similar design is pictured in the 1793 record of Gillow and Sons. The splayed legs, a feature that appeared about this time, add strength to slender designs. On the opposite page is a detail of lyre, trumpets, sun, and putti on the black background.

G E R M A N Y
AUSTRIA AND SWITZERLAND

By the end of the Middle Ages, the painted decoration of furniture in Europe had become a singular, congruous element in a broad sweeping current of colorful ornamentation. Painted miniatures, radiant altarpieces, luminous stained-glass windows, and the walls of humble and princely residences were illuminated, sometimes brilliantly, through the ever-more refined talents of artisan-painters. By the early sixteenth century, these craftsmen had begun to borrow from the sophisticated repertoire of the great European masters, and distinctive regional schools started to flower—spurred by trade with the Orient and the vicissitudes of fashion, and advanced by an intrepid corps of masterful colorists.

The eighteenth century, most notably from 1750 onward, was the epoch of European furniture painting, and this was true for Germany as well. Josef M. Ritz, in his study of painted furniture styles, regards this art as a communion of ornament and color, which, whether elegant or of modest pretensions, was universally loved.

Bedroom furniture dominates the pantheon of painted furniture from German-speaking lands: The armoire shown in a detail opposite, from the Salzburger Museum, would have been the prized possession of the Alsatian bride in 1841, the date of its inscription. Another armoire, this one from the Pinzgau region of Austria, is pictured in the detail inset above. Testifying to the regional preference for religious themes, the late Baroque period Austrian bed at the right features a pietà scene of a later date on the headboard and a profuse decoration of forget-me-nots and other symbolic blossoms on its serpentine footboard.

The son of the designer wrote on the reverse of this watercolor that the room was a salon intended for the prince of Hesse and that it was drawn before 1792. The painted panels presumably represent two of the seasons. The decoration on the pilasters typifies the "pointed oval" and cameo profiles that were to become so popular early in the next century. Characteristic of the precision of German designers, the sofa, dado, and paneling are in exact alignment. From the Cooper-Hewitt Museum, New York

At the same time it was produced according to strict disciplines throughout the German-speaking lands. The great centers were in the Bavarian Alps, Franconia, the Alpine regions of Austria including the Tyrol, the Appenzell region of Switzerland, Alsace and the Vosges, Saxony, and Silesia.

The first painted domestic furniture in Germany probably appeared about 1600 in Bavaria, which became a predominant center for the art. Early pieces, which are now very rare, were simple; their ornamentation consisted at first of stars and roses drawn with a compass, then black arabesques and floral designs stenciled directly onto untreated wood. Gradually the stencils and compasses were abandoned, the painting became more elaborate, the colors brightened, and the range of subjects expanded to include figures and scenes as well as stylized plant and floral motifs.

Painted backgrounds became increasingly popular during the later seventeenth century. According to documents of the period, the practice was introduced to permit the use of poorer-quality woods, particularly soft woods such as pine, which were unsuitable for sculpture carving. Regulations eventually prohibited

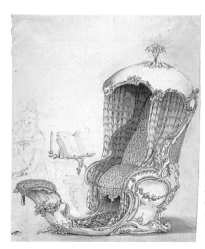

Insuring that the gentleman did not become bored on his journey, the sedan chair in the eighteenth-century watercolor at the left is fitted with a reading stand and candle. From the Cooper-Hewitt Museum, New York

From the abbey of Saint Florian comes one of the most elaborate examples of German Rococo painted furniture ever produced. A night's sleep in the carved bed above, supported by soldiers and open-shirted, turbaned companions, and surmounted by expressive putti, must have inspired curious dreams. Made about 1740. An equally grotesque and amusing painted object is the sled below, from the Salzburger Museum, made in Salzburg in the eighteenth century. The half-horse, half-sea-monster leaps dramatically from a dark, turbulent sea, and the jester perched at the front of the runners looks suitably intimidated by the icy plunge he is about to make.

the abuse of this technique: a 1660 guild rule in the Bavarian town of Tölz forbade carpenters to cover furniture with white lead, which might conceal flaws in the wood or joinery. Nevertheless, the prevalence of painting increased, although some areas continued to produce the old-fashioned designs on raw wood.

The armoire, introduced into middle-class homes and farmhouses in the seventeenth century, presented the best surface for painting, with divided panels that could be used for elaborate floral arrangements or different scenes of a story.

Some scholars link the rising popularity of painted furniture in these regions to the invasion of the mid-seventeenth-century style of art and architecture known as Baroque. Characterized by grand scale, luxuriance, and graceful curving forms, the Baroque movement began in Italy in the early seventeenth century and reached Germany soon after. The Rococo style, the ornate and lavish successor to the Baroque, introduced a number of new motifs, and the

Neoclassical influence brought subdued and disciplined color schemes into decoration. The tradition of painted furniture continued to gain in strength through the eighteenth century, when master cabinetmakers and designers produced pieces that spread their reputations far beyond their own towns and villages. Two such masters, Anton Porthaler de Degendorf and Johann Michael Russler de Untermunkeim, were widely known for their finely painted surfaces and lustrous hues. The most popular pieces of furniture were

A carved and painted Austrian coffer of about 1840 from the Pinzgau region serves as an entry hall table in a modern home, where it displays a collection of pewterware.

On the opposite page, a fine example of the early style of stenciling designs on raw wood, this Austrian armoire with a geometric pattern in black and reddish brown dates to 1683.

On these two pages are the
two sides of the painted furniture tradition: the chair
below is one of a pair of
eighteenth-century Dutch
painted armchairs in the folk
tradition, with rush seats;
the watercolor designs on
the opposite page of Ger-
man and Austrian chairs
with upholstered seats show
the influence of international Neoclassical trends of the
early nineteenth century.
Cooper-Hewitt Museum,
New York

even mass-produced, and in the finest workshops demand exceeded supply. But in the middle of the nineteenth century, this art ceased abruptly. Despite fine workmanship German painted furniture was primarily a folk art, and when popular taste shifted among the lower and middle classes to more somber ornamentation—leatherbound books, dark draperies, and muted paintings—the prosperous reign of painted furniture came to a close.

COLOR

Once the use of background colors was firmly established in the seventeenth century, green became the most frequently used hue, followed by black, which was particularly favored in Upper Austria. Four colors—white, blue-gray, brown, and reddish brown—predominated in the color schemes of the early eighteenth century, balanced in a rich and varied harmony; blue was also important at this time. With the advent of Neoclassicism at mid-century, the palette became muted, broadening to include

The pair of German painted and parcel-gilt wall brackets of the mid-eighteenth century at the left is unusual for the form of its seven candleholders, each in the shape of a different human head. On the opposite page the repentant Prodigal Son is greeted by his father in a scene from the desk below.

Like the painters of German-speaking lands, the Dutch often favored pious subjects. Lest the owner of this eighteenth-century desk forget the source of its decoration, the painter has included the scripture reference, Luke XV. Each side depicts a different part of the story of the Prodigal Son; the most vivid is the panel that shows the son sharing a meal of husks with swine.

The reason for the elaborate
fantasy of floral and wood-
land decoration on this corner settee becomes clear
when the source is known: it
was made for the summer
residence of Adam Friedrich
von Seinsheim, prince-
bishop of Würzburg and
Bamberg, at Seehof Castle.
Part of a set that included
another matching settee,
two armchairs, and four side
chairs, the settee is carved of
pine, painted, gilded, and
upholstered in a painted
satin made in China for the
Western market. It is now in
the Metropolitan Museum of
Art, New York.

The undulating front and sides of the German commode above of about 1765 suggest that its creator had seen the painted bombé commodes made in Venice in the mid-eighteenth century. Like the settee (left) the commode comes from Seehof Castle and is now in the collection of the Metropolitan Musuem of Art, New York.

The chair at the right is similar to the one on page 124. Both are of country origin, with caned seats and straight backs, and would have been suitable for everyday use.

A charming country chair, perhaps a milking stool, represents a man and woman kissing. Salzburger Museum, Salzburg

shades of gray and pale green. By the end of the eighteenth century, when the painter's art was perhaps at its most refined in these areas, the colors were lively but elegant, never lacking in delicacy or becoming garish. As painted furniture lost its cachet at the beginning of the nineteenth century, however, colors became dense and less carefully chosen. Germanic furniture is particularly characterized by its attention to contrast between artfully juxtaposed colors; the expressive greens and blues against reds and yellows give these pieces a singular intensity.

MOTIFS

Rococo embellishments of the early eighteenth century brought to painted furniture the element of fantasy. Roses, tulips, carnations, bellflowers, and leafy borders and clusters of all descriptions were transformed by painters into imaginary gardens of delight. In most floral decoration, the blossoms themselves dwarfed stems and leaves. Flowers bloomed on every surface, and specific floral decoration became identified with particular areas. The rose enjoyed a special place in the hearts of Alpine painters. There were the "little rose" of Tölz in Bavaria and the lush blossoms of the Black Forest clocks. In East Prussia flowers were the only motifs to be painted on furniture. The tulip, a flower imported from the Orient and first used on furniture from Augsburg in Bavaria, was prized by many, both open

and closed, probably for its meaning as a symbol of the Trinity. The painters' favorite use of flowers, however, was in lavish bunches or arrangements in vases, nearly overflowing with abundance. This effective ornamental treatment descended from Renaissance motifs first used on aristocratic or middle-class pieces in Bavaria. By the eighteenth century, the floral repertoire of painters had grown to include delicate local species of wildflowers. In some regions—Aloes, in the Zillertaler Alps, or in the Alpbachtal, for example—floral motifs were frequently combined with animals and birds.

In addition to these intimate views of nature were a number of landscapes, cityscapes, and figural scenes, many with religious content, which first appeared toward the end of the seventeenth and beginning of the eighteenth centuries. An oft-repeated composition was the town gate and a four-towered city, an image that derived from Italian sculpted-wood marquetry, prevalent in Bavaria and the Tyrol, particularly in the eighteenth century. There were Rococo

Following pages: Even as late as 1820, when this chest was made, simple painted furniture was the mainstay of household furnishings in rural homes. From the Salzburger Museum, Salzburg

A wealthy farmer would have commissioned this mid-eighteenth century Alpine armoire with its elaborate allegorical figures of Europe, Africa, Asia, and America on its door panels. The theme of the continents has been part of pictorial tradition since ancient times. A detail from a later Austrian armoire—of about 1813—is at the right. From the Salzburger Museum, Salzburg

landscapes featuring an abundant—though impossible in nature—array of exotic animals and vigorous flora. Figural arrangements can most often be found in the Alps and the Alpine foreland. Secular scenes include the four seasons—often neatly divided by the four panels of an armoire—fieldwork, a wedding feast, and dances. These celebrated stories of peasants and gardeners are known from popular songs and the theater. Religious themes were taken from the Bible or the lives of the saints. Portraits of Jesus and Mary, showing their hearts exposed, or the hearts themselves as pious symbols, were especially highly regarded. Artists usually derived inspiration for these images from their local churches.

ALSACE

In technique and color, the painted furnishings of Alsace resemble those of the other German-speaking areas, but they were generally more somber than the furniture of Switzerland, Bavaria, or the Scandinavian countries. And perhaps more than in other

A colorful combination of birds and fruit enlivens this simple Austrian chair of the nineteenth century.

Two armoires represent two regional styles. The one at the left is from the Austrian Pinzgau region; the armoire on the opposite page comes from Passau and dates to about 1825. It is part of an ensemble that includes the bed on the following page.

Das Bild hier stellt uns vor, den flug der schnellen Zeit:
Durch Zukunft, Gegenwart, und auch Vergangenheit.

Geh laß den Segel aus, und sper ihn doch nicht ein,
Du weißt wie karl es ist, wenn du mußt afangen seim.

Lebt luftig und seyd froh, in euer Jugend Zeit
Doch freuet euch nur so, daß euch nie gereut!

Das Unschuldvolle kindliche Alter.

Das gefährvolle Jugendliche Alter.

Das Sorgenvolle Männliche Alter.

Das gebrechliche hohe Alter.

Wer mühesam ist und treibt, was ihm von Gott beschieden
Dem fehlts an Gottes Seegen nicht, und lebt allzeit zufrie-
den.

Gesang und Saitenspiel, ist für mich eitelkeit
Weill es bald heißen wird, fort in die Ewigkeit.

Amor

die Liebe.

Fortuna

das Glück.

By the date of this yellow-painted bed, about 1825, German and Austrian furniture design had come under the pervasive influence of the Empire style. Still this piece retains its traditional flavor: typical of such beds, the headboard pictures a religious motif and the footboard a domestic scene, in this case a family engaged in removing the lice from each other's heads.

lands, in Alsace painted furniture took on a special cultural significance—it was the most important part of the bride's dowry and her only possession for the first years of married life. The usual ensemble, designed to match in color and decoration, included an armoire, a canopied bed, a chest, a kitchen sideboard that was combination larder and cupboard, a few chairs, a cradle, and a corner cupboard. In the nineteenth century, a chest of drawers sometimes joined the group.

Alsatian eighteenth-century cabinetmakers, and also those from nearby regions, employed a unique method for painting their furniture, which produced interesting effects. Once the background had been painted brown, part of it was rubbed while the paint was still wet, yielding a transparent glaze over the wood. Around the middle of the eighteenth century, a variation was introduced: the artist used a cloth pad to create a mottled or antiqued surface. In the nineteenth century, the perfect finishing tool was discovered to be a cut potato dipped in brown ocher, beer, and vinegar. The starch of the potato became a binder, replacing the need for the earlier milk-and-wheat-glue mixture.

Among other background treatments of the region were mottled and marbleized surfaces, favored in the Lower Rhine, and blue, turquoise, and bluish green in the Upper Rhine. Brown and reddish brown backgrounds are also found in simulation of veneered wood or marquetry, and there are also stenciled motifs similar to those found in some of the other German-speaking areas. Unfortunately, these techniques died out with the decline of painted furniture internationally, at the end of the nineteenth century.

Armoires of the Zillertaler region, near the Tyrol, nearly always have green-painted fronts and brown-painted sides without decoration, as seen in the detail at the left from an eighteenth-century example. The painted pine armoire at the right, called a *Vogelkasten*, was made in the Alpine region of southern Austria called Styria and dates to about 1810.

S W E D E N
A N D   D E N M A R K

Two important traditions of painted furniture developed in Sweden: the high-style aristocratic furniture that evolved from the international taste for oriental lacquer beginning in the seventeenth century; and the rural folk tradition, which grew up both in the manors of landowners (where it attempted to imitate its elegant counterpart) and in humble peasant dwellings. As late as the seventeenth century the great houses of Sweden were still closed fortresses—large rectangular structures furnished

with imposing, simple chairs and tables. Tastes began to change by the end of the century when the architects Nicodemus Tessin and his son Nicodemus traveled to Italy, where they eagerly embraced the refined luxury of Italian and French styles. As the designers of Drottningholm Castle and the grand castle at Stockholm, the Tessins did much to spread the appreciation of sumptuous, high Baroque decoration among the Swedish nobility.

Scandinavian style in painted furniture encompassed a range of influences and variations. The Danish intimacy with the court of France resulted in the chair in the Louis XVI style at the left, from the collection of Anton Kristansen. The detail of a Swedish cupboard from Västerbotten on the opposite page betrays a hint of Rococo influence in its curving outlines. The cupboard, in the Nordiska Museet, Stockholm, is attributed to Per Olof Hallin. Another Swedish cupboard (detail in inset above), signed by Hans Wikström and dated 1793, comes from the Gästrikland region and is also in the Nordiska Museet.

During the epoch known as the "Caroline" after the three kings named Karl—Charles X, XI, and XII, who ruled from 1654 to 1718—not only furniture but even walls and ceilings were enriched with painted murals, often in the new French style named after the *ornamentiste* Jean Bérain, who employed the delicate technique of grisaille. The true Swedish Rococo style came to full flowering about 1740 under the influence of the French. So engaged was the Swedish aristocracy with France and its fashions that they spoke and wrote French—even for official government business—rather than their Scandinavian tongue. Among the most fashionable designs of the period were wooden wardrobes with panels painted in the style of Madame de Pompadour's favorite painter, François Boucher. Hunt scenes and pastoral vignettes often included a number of charming, if unrealistic, figures dressed in knee breeches and country frocks, chatting under perfectly shaped trees in ideal landscapes. Chinoiserie was as important to Rococo taste in Sweden as it was in France,

Few monuments to the love affair between eighteenth-century Europe and China are as impressive as the Chinese Pavilion at Drottningholm Castle near Stockholm. The structure that stands in the castle's park today was not the first to be built. The original pavilion, a gift to Queen Ulrika from her husband King Adolf Frederick on her thirty-third birthday, was erected and decorated in 1753. Although greatly admired, the pavilion was replaced little more than a decade later, when the royal architect Carl Frederick Adelcrantz was commissioned to build a new "China." Seeking inspiration from the Chinese pavilion in Rheinsberg and the Japanese Haus in Potsdam, he created a structure that, inside and outside, reflects the Rococo style. The Green Salon, pictured here, at the end of the East Wing, features a set of black and gold stools upholstered in the original green leather. Made in 1767, they testify to the close connections between Stockholm and Paris and are important forerunners of the Neoclassical style.

147

The Rococo style quickly became established in the Swedish Jämtland, because its inhabitants often studied in Stockholm. This cupboard from Järvsö, dated 1793, shows the talent of the Jämtland painters, who decorated homes and churches as well as furniture. Nordiska Museet, Stockholm

and lacquerware with oriental subject matter became increasingly popular. Chinese porcelain imported by the Swedish East India Company inspired affection for things Chinese. The Chinese Pavilion at Drottningholm is an example of the Swedish passion for this taste.

With the end of the Rococo era came the style called Gustavian after Gustavus III, who seized power in 1771. This was the Swedish interpretation of the classical revival that swept Europe beginning in 1760 and which lasted nearly to the middle of the nineteenth century. The marvelous pavilion at Haga, the summer home of Swedish royalty designed by the architect Olof Templeman, contains excellent examples of painted murals in the Gustavian style and many fine examples of painted furniture with delicate columns, fluting, and other restrained Neoclassical

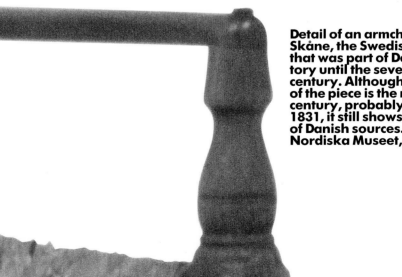

Detail of an armchair from Skåne, the Swedish province that was part of Danish territory until the seventeenth century. Although the date of the piece is the nineteenth century, probably about 1831, it still shows influence of Danish sources. From the Nordiska Museet, Stockholm

ornaments. Although the curves of Rococo did not altogether vanish, persisting in some form throughout the eighteenth century, the progression of Swedish style was unmistakably severe. In the final phase of this style, the Gustavian chairs closely resembled the original antique models that had inspired them, with klismos-style curved backs and saber legs—also characteristic of the French Empire style.

The Empire style soon invaded Sweden directly, when Napoleon's marshal Jean-Baptiste-Jules Bernadotte became its ruler, and ultimately its king, Charles XIV, in 1818. The arrival of Empire mahogany furniture with gilt ormolu fittings soon eclipsed and finally supplanted painted furniture.

Porcelain figures line the shelves of the cabinet and appear as well all along the top border of this room from the Drottningholm Chinese Pavilion.

Many of the Swedish painted furniture pieces are cupboards like this one. Made in about 1790 in Jämtland, it is attributed to Anders Berglin. Nordiska Museet, Stockholm

THE FOLK TRADITION

Perhaps even more than in the castles of kings, in country manors and farmhouses painted furniture was a keynote of decoration. The earliest examples, dating to about 1595, come from the region of Hälsingborg, where farmers had acquired enough wealth to construct fine residences and fill them with specially commissioned furniture. By the eighteenth and nineteenth centuries, painted furniture could be found in almost every region of Sweden, although it was more popular in some areas than others. In the same tradition as folk furniture from all over Scandinavia, Austria, Germany, and Eastern Europe, painted furniture from the Swedish countryside followed, but did not directly parallel, international trends in cabinet-making.

The central province of Dalecarlia produced the largest number of pieces, which were often the most original. Walls were frequently painted to blend with the schemes of furniture ensembles. Beginning in the early seventeenth century, Dalecarlian painters most often used the acanthus motif in their designs. As painting techniques gained popularity toward the

A cupboard attributed to Per Olof Hallin, Vasterbotten, Sweden, now in the Nordiska Museet, Stockholm

153

mid-eighteenth century, certain painters achieved recognition—Hans Erson Enman was perhaps the best known. Under the influence of the Baroque, Swedish painting styles became more ornate, acquiring the nickname *kurbitsmåleri* from the Swedish word for gourd—no doubt a reference to the sinuous lines of Baroque painting. An especially exciting variation of the Baroque style named after the artist Erik Eliasson featured flowers painted in carmine, blue, or white against a maroon ground. The blossoms were brushed on with a light wash of color, which permitted the background to show through, giving a powerful impression of three-dimensionality. At its height after 1770, the Eliasson style declined early in the next century when painters began to take shortcuts in the laborious technique. Maroon backgrounds were dropped in favor of blue and green.

The trio of Swedish cupboards here spans more than a half-century and represents three provinces. The example at the left, signed by Hans Wikström and dated 1793, comes from Gästrikland. Above, a cupboard made in 1824 by the Haga School of painters in Jämtland. Both are in the collection of the Nordiska Museet, Stockholm.

Dalecarlia produced not only lavish furniture and wall hangings, but also scythes and grindstones for distribution in other Swedish provinces and export to Norway and Finland. This cupboard, dated 1849 and signed Mats Persson Stadig, was used to store milk. Nordiska Museet, Stockholm

Skåne (Scania), the south-ernmost region of Sweden, had painted furniture traditions of its own, largely derived from those of Denmark, since it was a Danish province until 1658. Southern pieces, primarily blanket chests and armoires, featured Rococo and Baroque decoration with rose-bushes heavily laden with bloom. The Erik Eliasson style of painting spread from Dalecarlia to Skåne at the end of the eighteenth century, intermingling with the southern style.

Other regions invented their own designs. Painters from Delsbo or Järvsö, in the Dellen Lake district, notably Gustavus Reuter, originated a version of Baroque-style painting that was free of influence from other areas. In Jämtland (bordering Norway), the armoires, in typically Rococo style, were particularly interesting. In some areas along the sea-coast, such as Blekinge, painted furniture was a rarity.

Working within the constraints of established designs, the maker of the blue-painted chairs in the Confidence Room of the Chinese Pavilion at Drottningholm (opposite page) carved the seats so that they rested directly on the legs, without an intervening rail for support—thus producing an exotic variation through economical means. Chinoiserie found another outlet in the rare longcase clock at the right, made about 1765 by Nils Berg, whose signature appears on the case.

DENMARK

France, England and Holland all had their influences on the development of Denmark's interior decoration style. Like those countries, Denmark caught the passion for lacquer from the wares imported from China beginning in the seventeenth century. Danish craftsmen then copied Chinese motifs: about 1616, for example, Samuel Clausen decorated one of the rooms of the Rosenborg Castle in Copenhagen in the

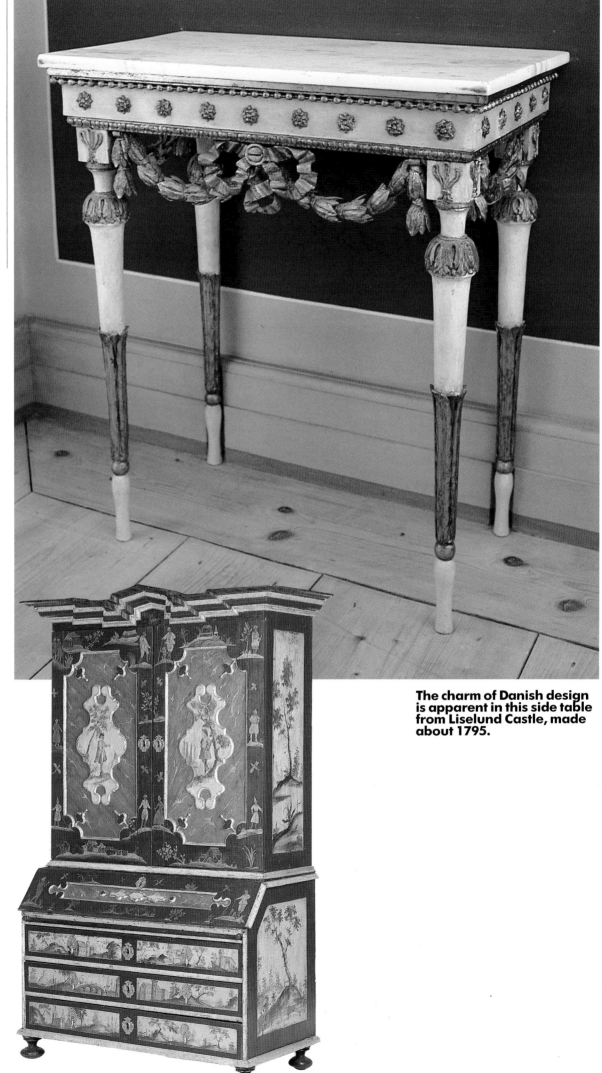

The charm of Danish design is apparent in this side table from Liselund Castle, made about 1795.

At the right is an early Danish painted bureau of about 1720. The chair on the opposite page is, like the side table above, from Liselund Castle. Made in about 1800, it shows a strong influence of English Neoclassical design.

Chinese style; it is thought to be the earliest room in Europe to be outfitted in chinoiserie.

Painted furniture continued to be fashionable throughout the seventeenth and eighteenth centuries, at first following the trends established by the French. The Régence style, so called after Philippe, duke of Orleans, the regent for Louis XV from 1715 to 1723, predominated early in the century, but painted furniture reached its height during the Baroque, Rococo, and Neoclassical periods that ensued. The upper classes even took up the painting of furniture as a stylish hobby. Nonetheless, most painted furniture came from professional firms, which produced goods of extremely high quality. A desk manufactured by one of these companies, Ronnings Laker of Copenhagen, now in the National Museum of Copenhagen, represents the transitional period between the Régence and Rococo styles.

Liselund Castle was built on Møn Island in 1795 for Antoine de la Calmette, the son of a French ambassador posted to Denmark in 1760. Influenced by the philosophy of Jean-Jacques Rousseau, young Calmette laid out an idyllic park around his château. Designed with exquisite taste, the decor of Liselund Castle, as well as its architecture and handsome grounds, have earned it the nickname Petit Trianon of Denmark. At the left is a settee from Liselund Castle, about 1800, and on the following pages is one of the castle's salons.

Rococo appeared in Denmark about 1740, showing evidence of its journey across the continent: French, German, and even English influences can be seen in its curves, shells, and curlicues. The most popular color for painted furniture at this time was red, followed by white and green, often edged in gold.

The English mode next dominated Danish style, in the pale colors and straight lines of Hepplewhite and Sheraton, whose pattern books met with the same enthusiasm in Denmark as they had elsewhere in Europe. These readily available drawings, along with high import tariffs, encouraged the growth of the furniture industry in Denmark, and by the first half of the nineteenth century Danish cabinetmakers could supply aristocratic residences with plentiful renditions of English-style painted chairs and other furnishings.

was as sturdy as wood. After obtaining a patent, Clay set up a business in Birmingham in 1793 that was to be one of the most important Midlands industries for the next century. Beginning with trays—some of which are the finest examples of japanned ware ever produced—Clay soon went on to furnishings, primarily tables for serving tea. The earliest of these was round, with a single pedestal leg and a rotating top. Later, Clay and other manufacturers issued papier-mâché sets of four tables, along with dressing tables, gaming tables, sewing tables, and, on rare occasions, papier-mâché beds. Countless smaller objects were produced, including Clay's famous trays: in his King Street shop in London, he created an entire line of papier-mâché trays, each model with its own name.

Lacquer finishes with chinoiserie were especially suitable for papier-mâché, but the versatility of the material lent itself to embellishments of flowers, landscapes, country scenes, animals—and sometimes even portraits. The most extravagant examples had gilding and inlay, most frequently mother-of-pearl. Whatever the design, the best makers hand-polished their finishes, producing a deep, lustrous patina.

The vogue for papier-mâché persisted throughout Europe until 1860, but it was perhaps the most pervasive in England, where Clay's process and Victorian taste combined to insure its success. As attested in a report from the Exposition Universelle in Paris of 1855, English love of papier-mâché led to English mastery of the medium: "The examples exhibited by the

Papier-mâché from two countries shows the versatility of this material. The English tray above, in the shape called Gothic, presents a peaceful scene of gentlefolk beside the water—an "Italian" landscape bathed in golden Mediterranean light. Below is a nineteenth-century Viennese desk with mother-of-pearl inlay and a leather top. The malleability of papier-mâché encouraged exaggeration of certain forms, such as the legs of the desk.

French and the Germans show a great deal of refinement, but the products from Birmingham are superior in all respects to those of other countries." Comparing "an object of [the firm] Jennens and Bettridge" to a Prussian one, another report concluded that "the superiority of the former is incontestable." Jennens and Bettridge, which replaced Clay's firm as the leading factory in the Birmingham area, had earned a reputation for the finest wares in Europe by this date, but ironically the company closed its doors just nine years later, when changing tastes and the industrial revolution conspired to withdraw public favor from papier-mâché in Europe.

In America, where the first papier-mâché factory opened only in the early 1850s, the Litchfield Manufacturing Company of Litchfield, Connecticut, employed more than fifty workers, primarily engaged in fabricating the casings of clocks, rather than trays or furniture. Quality was not as high as it was in England, however, and the factory closed about 1854.

The chiffonier on the opposite page is made of ebonized pearwood and papier-mâché, with mother-of-pearl inlay and floral decoration. The style is typical of the Napoleon III period, of about 1860. Musée des Arts Décoratifs, Paris. Above is an English papier-mâché tray of Gothic outline with a peacock design, probably made in Birmingham about 1820. Below: Papier-mâché persisted into the late nineteenth century in England, the origin of this Rococo-revival style chair inlaid with mother-of-pearl.

CARE OF PAINTED FURNITURE

By following a few simple guidelines, the owners of painted furniture can maintain the beauty of their prized pieces forever.

The greatest enemies of painted furniture, as with all fine antiques, are rapid fluctuations in temperature and humidity, direct sunlight, and carelessness.

Changes in temperature and humidity have by far the greatest potential for damage, causing cracking, splitting, warping, and chipping. American homes in particular are notorious for hot dry air in the winter and blasts of cold dry air in the summer. Either extreme is drastically different from the usual European conditions—a constant cooler temperature and lightly moist air. Naturally there is variation in any home atmosphere, and furniture "breathes" to accommodate such changes. But because layers of French polish, varnish, paint, veneer, and wood base all expand and contract at different rates, it is essential that pieces newly imported from abroad be slowly introduced to the new environment. Vacillations in temperature and humidity are as detrimental as the presence of hot, dry air, or excessively wet, cool air.

The best conditions for painted furniture are a stable, slightly cool temperature, and moist, constant humidity. Painted furniture must never be placed next to a radiator, hot-air vent, air conditioner, or open window. The best position is against an inside wall, out of drafts and traffic, where conditions can be controlled. Humidifiers are useful in winter, as long as mist does not fall directly on the furniture itself.

Fine furniture should never be placed in direct sunlight. Not only does light cause fading, but the painted finish can also blur as layers of varnish shift. Should this occur, the situation is easily remedied by repositioning the piece away from direct sunlight. Under the care of a professional restorer, the old layers of varnish can be removed, reviving the color and patina of the original finish.

One of the major—though easily avoided—hazards to furniture is careless handling. Here, common sense is the rule. Vacuum cleaners must be carefully manipulated to avoid denting legs and chipping paint. Small children need to be taught the value of family treasures— that they are to be used, but with care. One must also keep a watchful eye on household pets. All antiques, of course, should be protected from liquids, hot plates, and other possible sources of surface damage.

Furniture purchased from a reliable auction house or dealer should be structurally sound, but the joints of any piece can weaken if abused. Heat not only destroys painted surfaces, but also dries wood glue and shrinks interlocking parts, causing joints to buckle and warp. In moving heavy furniture, never drag it or lean it to one side. This practice will at the least strain the framework and at the worst may snap a leg. Remove the drawers, fragile hardware, and heavy marble tops before carefully lifting the frame.

Occasionally antiques may become afflicted with woodworm. Today this malady is uncommon; the wormholes on the undersides, rails, and legs of some pieces usually indicate an infestation of the past. Be alert, however, for yellowish deposits around the tiny holes, the sign of active larvae burrowing inside the wood. Woodworm is easily eradicated by a professional restorer.

For everyday care, painted furniture should be lightly dusted with a soft dry cloth. Harsh chemicals and spray polishes are to be avoided, since they may build up on the surface and cause it to dull. Feather dusters are not recommended, since they may catch on a loose splinter or a flake of paint and lift it from the surface. Hard-to-reach crevices and problem spots—such as loose inlay or marquetry—may be cleaned lightly with a fine, soft brush.

Furniture need be waxed no more than once or twice a year, since the cleaning and buffing will keep it polished in the intervals. Natural oils and waxes are the best polishes; I prefer butcher's wax. After first dusting the piece thoroughly, apply a small amount of wax with a wad of barely damp cheesecloth. Wait about twenty minutes, then rub vigorously in a circular motion until all traces of wax have disappeared and the surface glows with a deep luster.

Lacquers and some types of paint may crackle beneath the polished surface. This condition, which adds the charm of age to a fine piece, need not be cause for alarm, unless the lacquer is actively flaking away. In this case the finish should be left undisturbed until a restorer can examine and treat it. Gilded surfaces, as well as ormolu mounts, should be handled

with special care, since, whether the gilt is gold leaf or gold-colored paint, the layer is often quite thin. If the surface has worn away to expose the gesso or bronze beneath, the ornament should be restored by a professional rather than touched up with gold paint, which is likely to be of a noticeably different color than the original finish. Even more than other materials, gilt and ormolu are highly vulnerable to damage from water. Never attempt to clean them with water-based cleaners.

The care of papier-mâché and painted metal is much the same as that for painted wood. Unless exposed to excessive moisture, papier-mâché is a durable material, but larger pieces should be delicately handled, since they are more fragile than wood. With painted metals, the main danger is from rust, which may attack iron and steel once the surface has been chipped away. If used for table service, trays of *tôle peinte* should be protected from wet objects and spills. Serious rusting should be referred to a restorer.

Despite these cautionary notes, it should be remembered that painted furniture is no more difficult to maintain and preserve than any fine antique. It should be enjoyed as well as cherished. Simple attention and care will preserve fine pieces not only for your own use, but for the pleasure of generations to come.

GLOSSARY

ACANTHUS
An ornate leafy decoration borrowed from classical Greek furniture by Rococo artists. Corinthian capitals are decorated with clusters of acanthus leaves.

ADAM STYLE
The architect Robert Adam and his brother James revolutionized furniture and interior design in mid-eighteenth century England with their interpretation of the Neoclassical style. In it, they sought to harmonize the architecture of a house with its interior.

ANTHEMION
A flower motif borrowed from the ancient Greeks by Neoclassical craftsmen.

BAROQUE
The Baroque style, sumptuously embellishing all it touched with flowers, leafy borders, arabesques, and chinoiserie, appeared first in Italy in the middle of the seventeenth century. Highly ornate and somewhat pompous, it was intended initially to reflect the riches of the Roman Catholic Church. Marked by the influence of architects and sculptors, Baroque furniture is heavily sculpted and on a grand scale.

BEECHWOOD
Considered an inferior wood by the English, light-colored beech was commonly used but most often covered with gilding, paint, or lacquer.

BOMBÉ
(Literally "bulging").
A French term used to describe the shape of commodes popular during the Baroque period.

CABRIOLE
A chair leg that curves outward at the knee and then tapers to the carved foot. This S-shape of the cabriole leg is a trademark of the Rococo style.

CHINOISERIE
The term for European adaptations of Chinese arts such as lacquer, porcelain, and oriental decorating motifs. The fad for Chinese imitations reached its height early in the eighteenth century, and was perfectly suited to the lighthearted vibrancy of the Rococo style, after which it subsided somewhat to be revived again in Victorian England.

CHIPPENDALE STYLE
The influence of the *Gentleman and Cabinet-Maker's Director* (1754) by the furniture maker Thomas Chippendale was so great that English Rococo is sometimes called "Chippendale style." Trans-

lated into French and Italian, the *Director's* illustrations of nearly every type of furniture design spread English fashion throughout Europe. Not only was his name given to the broad English style, but to variations of it as well—Rococo sprinkled with chinoiserie became Chinese Chippendale, and furniture designs using medieval motifs and lofty architectural forms were known as Chippendale Gothic. Although famous for these highly elaborate Rococo adaptations, some of Chippendale's finest and subtlest later work was in the Neoclassical style, when he designed interiors with Robert Adam.

DEPENTORI
Italian lacquerers.

EBONY/EBONIZING
An exotic dark wood, ebony was often imitated by ebonizing, the staining of light woods, such as pearwood.

EMPIRE STYLE
The Empire style was molded by Napoleon himself to reflect the extent and might of his rule. Its lines are massive and the decoration is lavish, marked often by Napoleon's particular motifs—the bee, wreaths, eagles, and the letter N. Echoes of classical styles were carefully cultivated to draw a parallel between the Roman and Napoleonic Empires.

FAUX MARBRE
A trompe l'oeil effect that imitates marble, *faux marbre*—or marbling—was particularly popular among the flamboyant Venetians.

GESSO
A thick paste of plaster of Paris and size, gesso was applied to furniture in heavy layers and then carved, painted, or gilded.

GRISAILLE
A very delicate trompe l'oeil finish that simulated relief carving through the manipulation of shades of gray paint.

GROTESQUES
Ornamental carvings or paintings of fantastic creatures—griffins, sphinxes, distorted human figures—as well as of fanciful natural shapes—plants, flowers, and birds. Grotesques were particularly popular among Baroque and Rococo artists.

HEPPLEWHITE STYLE
In the patterns of his book *The Cabinet-Maker and Upholsterer's Guide* (1788), which circulated widely among country craftsmen in England, George Hepplewhite paired the elegance of the Adam style with a utilitarian quality. Falling between the early Neoclassicism of Adam and the fully matured variation of Sheraton, Hepplewhite's style is simple but elegant, often marked by his trademark motifs—the Prince of Wales feathers and wheat ears.

JAPANNING
The term most often used by the English for the European adaptation of oriental lacquering.

KLISMOS
As the curves of cabriole legs had appealed to Rococo tastes, the simple lines of this ancient Greek chair inspired Neoclassical artisans. Elegant with sleek contours, the klismos has a gently curved back leading to saber legs.

LACCA CONTRAFATTA
More economical than French or English lacquerers, the Italian *depentori* devised an imitation of the oriental art that eliminated the need for painstaking brushwork. Instead of painting each piece themselves, they used cut-outs of prints or engravings by popular artists which they then glued to the furniture surface and coated with layers of sandarac.

LACQUER
An oriental varnish in use as early as the first century to decorate furniture and small objects. Made from the sap of the *Rhus vernicifera*, a plant found only in the East, the lacquer was applied in many layers, each polished to a high gloss, and then carved in relief or painted.

MAHOGANY
When embellished with gilt and ormolu fittings, this majestic red wood was the quintessence of Napoleon's Empire style.

MARQUETRY
A veneer of various colored woods, bone, ivory, or mother-of-pearl, marquetry was used to decorate the surfaces of pieces such as commodes and tabletops. A shallow finish, it was easier to work with than the imbedded designs of inlay, which it more or less replaced, until marquetry too was largely overshadowed by painted furniture at the end of the eighteenth century.

NEOCLASSICAL STYLE
Simple forms and plain decoration of the Neoclassical style replaced the previous Rococo excesses. The austerity of the new style reflected the ideals of the French Revolution, and its subtle decorative treatment,

with clean crisp lines, was inspired by the recent archaeological discoveries from classical Rome.

OMEGA WORKSHOPS
Founded by the art critic Roger Fry to promote English decorative arts and as a showcase for several artists of the British Bloomsbury crowd, such as Vanessa Bell and Duncan Grant. The Omega artists decorated household objects—from textiles and pottery to furniture—with their simple designs in vivid colors.

ORMOLU
(Literally "ground gold").
Refers to the small figures cast in bronze and finished in a thin layer of gold leaf, which were used to decorate eighteenth- and nineteenth-century furniture.

PAPIER-MÂCHÉ
Discovered first in the Middle East, papier-mâché had been in use for centuries when it first reached France early in the eighteenth century. Malleable and surprisingly strong, papier-mâché, mixed with glue, chalk and sometimes sand, became a popular material for furniture which was then often japanned. The English were particularly enamored with the curious new method. Henry Clay ran an enormously successful papier-mâché business, and the Victorians perfected the art.

PATERA
A small, round Greek motif, often at the center of acanthus leaves or used in a series to decorate furniture in the Neoclassical style.

PENNSYLVANIA DUTCH
An early American decorative folk style developed by German settlers in Pennsylvania. The Pennsylvania Dutch adorned all household wares with their cheerful colors and trademark motifs—stars, tulips, trees of life, and hearts.

PERCIER AND FONTAINE
The two great eighteenth-century architects and designers Percier and Fontaine created the Empire style and molded it to reflect the wealth and splendor of the Napoleonic era. Not surprisingly, the emperor took them on as his per-

sonal architects, assuring the dissemination of their style—and thus his own reputation—through his extended court. Their Empire furniture was lavishly decorated with ormolu fittings and Napoleonic motifs, most often on rich, dark mahogany.

PONTYPOOL AND USK WARE
Near the end of the seventeenth century, in Pontypool, Wales, Thomas Allgood discovered a coal byproduct that could be adhered to metal by the application of heat and then painted. This new *tôle* method, which was made in factories in Pontypool and Usk, was very successful until replaced by a newer electroplating process.

QUEEN ANNE STYLE
This distinctively British branch of the Baroque developed during Queen Anne's reign (1702–14). It pared down the Baroque curves to simpler lines and discouraged sculpting and japanning.

RÉGENCE
The first phase of the Rococo, the Régence style (named after the French Prince Regent, Philippe d'Orleans, 1715–23), evolved in reaction against the self-conscious grandeur of the preceding Baroque. As interior decoration became more established, Régence designs began to lose the formal, architectural dependence of the previous style.

REGENCY
Regency artisans carried the antique motifs of the Neoclassical a step further by incorporating them into the actual antique styles. Embellished with scrolls and anthemions, furniture in addition took on the mass and elegance of Greek designs. The work of Thomas Hope is most characteristic of this style, named after the British Prince Regent who became George IV in 1820.

RESTAURATION
Though it marked the end of Napoleon and return of the French monarchy, the Restauration style did not vary significantly from the Empire except for somewhat lighter coloring and the predictable disappearance of Napoleonic motifs.

ROCOCO
Much more elegant and playful than the weighty Baroque, the Rococo style was more determined to delight than impress with its riches. Porcelain, lacquer, and other exotic imports found their places in the new style and were decorated with elaborate pastorals and natural motifs—splashes of water, shells, and designs borrowed from the rockwork of gardens—in French, *rocaille*—from which the style derives its name.

SATINWOOD
Unlike beech, this golden-colored wood was considered by the English to be of the best quality for furniture making and in a style distinctly their own, English craftsmen decorated it with delicately painted garlands of flowers and arabesques while at the same time leaving the natural wood color visible.

SANDARAC
A reddish, translucent varnish used as a substitute for the lacquer made only in the Orient.

SHERATON STYLE
A final phase of British Neoclassicism, the Sheraton style brought an Anglicized version of Parisian taste to a somewhat simplified Adam style. The creator of this school, Thomas Sheraton, published his designs in the influential *Cabinet-Maker and Upholsterer's Drawing-Book* (1791–94). His sophisticated though rather severe patterns, with classical motifs borrowed from Adam, were highly prized by American cabinetmakers of the Federal style.

TÔLE PEINTE
The French term for japanned metalware.

TROMPE L'OEIL
The use of painting to give the illusion of other media, trompe l'oeil finishes were particularly prevalent in eighteenth-century painted furniture. Artisans, perfecting the arts of grisaille, *faux marbre*, and ebonizing to simulate the textures and colors of relief carvings, marble, and wood, which may not always have been available, also discovered an ideal stage for showing off their craftsmanship.

VERNIS MARTIN
The finest imitation of oriental lacquer and a catalyst in the fashion of painted furniture, this distinctive varnish, enhanced by gold dust, was made popular in France by Robert, Guillaume, Simon-Etienne, and Julien Martin early in the eighteenth century.

WINDSOR STYLE
The name given to a large family of English chair design popular late in the seventeenth century. The many variations make it difficult to characterize, but all have saddle seats, slightly splayed seats and in the most popular variety—a back of spindles.

REFERENCES

Page 21, "inspired by the latest fashion": Pierre Kjellberg, *Le Mobilier français du moyen-âge à Louis XV* (Paris: Guy le Prat, 1978), vol. I, p. 134.

Page 22, col. 2 "Martin has surpassed the art of China"; "les panneaux sont de Martin vernis"; and "the carriages varnished by Martin": Quoted in Arsène Alexandre, *Histoire de l'art décoratif du 16ème siècle à nos jours* (Paris: H. Laurens, 1892), pp. 62, 69.

Page 25, col. 2, "painter then spreads onto the particular piece": Henry Havard, *Dictionnaire de l'ameublement,* 1890, s.v. Martin.

Page 35, col. 4, "the spirit, principles, and wisdom of antiquity" and "for the architect to be indifferent to them": Quoted in Kjellberg, *Le Mobilier français du style transition à l'art Déco,* vol. I, p. 159.

Page 62, col. 1, "the contours were well modulated": Saul Lévy, *Laques vénitiennes du 18ème siècle* (Paris: Société Française du Livre, 1968), vol. I, p. 15.

Page 85, "decorated by painting or gilding, or left in a plain state": Ralph Edwards, *The Dictionary of English Furniture* (1924; repr. ed. Woodbridge, England: Baron Publishing, 1983), vol. II, p. 266.

Page 93, col. 2, "Brown puick with Silver dust": Edwards, *The Dictionary of English Furniture,* vol. II, p. 268.

Page 109, col. 1, "the general hue of the chair": Quoted in Ralph Fastnedge, *Sheraton Furniture* (Woodbridge, England: Baron Publishing, 1983), p. 45.

Page 109, col. 1, Prussian blue, vermilion, and gray-green: Fastnedge, *Sheraton Furniture,* p. 46.

Page 109, col. 2, "painted blue and white": Edwards, *The Dictionary of English Furniture,* vol. III, p. 13.

Page 119, his study of painted furniture styles: Josef M. Ritz, *Alte bemalte Bauernmöbel* (Munich: Georg Callwey, 1938).

Page 189, col. 1, "former is incontestable": Jane Toller, *Papier-Mâché in Great Britain and America* (Newton, Massachusetts: C. T. Branford Co., 1962) p. 22.

BIBLIOGRAPHY

Alexandre, Arsène. *Histoire de l'art décoratif du 16ème siècle à nos jours.* Paris: H. Laurens, 1892.

Anscombe, Isabelle. *Omega and After: Bloomsbury and the Decorative Arts.* London: Thames and Hudson, 1981.

Baltimore Painted Furniture: 1800–1840. Baltimore: The Baltimore Museum of Art, 1972.

Barrielle, Jean-François. *Le Style empire.* Paris: Flammarion, 1982.

Bonanni, Filippo. *Trattato sopra la vernice communemente detta cinese.* Venice, 1720.

Cescinsky, Herbert. *English Furniture from Gothic to Sheraton.* New York: Dover Publications, Inc., 1968.

Chippendale, Thomas. *The Gentleman and Cabinet-Maker's Director.* London, 1754. 3d ed. New York: Dover Publications, 1966.

Christ, Yvan. *L'Art au XIXème siècle.* Paris: Flammarion, 1981.

Dossie, Robert. *Handmaid to the Arts.* London, 1758.

Edwards, Ralph. *The Dictionary of English Furniture.* Woodbridge, England: Baron Publishing, 1924.

Fabris, Annamaria Rispoli. *L'Arte della lacca.* Milan: Electa, 1974.

Fales, Dean A., and Robert Bishop. *American Painted Furniture: 1660–1880.* New York: E. P. Dutton, 1979.

Fastnedge, Ralph. *Sheraton Furniture.* Woodbridge, England: Baron Publishing, 1983.

Harris, Eileen. *The Furniture of Robert Adam.* London: Tiranti, 1963.

Havard, Henry. *Dictionnaire de l'ameublement.* Paris, 1880–90.

Hayward, Helen. *World Furniture.* London: Hamlyn Publishing Group, 1965.

Hepplewhite, George. *The Cabinet-Maker and Upholsterer's Guide.* London, 1788. 3d ed. New York: Dover Publications, 1969.

John, W. D., and Anne Simcox. *Pontypool and Usk Japanned Wares.* Bath, England: Harding and Curtis, 1984.

Kjellberg, Pierre. *Le Mobilier français du moyen-âge à Louis XV.* Paris: Guy le Prat, 1978.

————. *Le Mobilier français du style transition à l'art Déco.* Paris: Guy le Prat, 1980.

Lévy, Saul. *Laques vénitiennes du 18ème siècle.* Paris: Société Française du Livre, 1968.

Lucie-Smith, Edward. *Furniture.* London: Thames and Hudson, 1979.

Manners, Lady Victoria, et al. *Angelica Kauffmann.* London: The Bodley Head, 1924.

Mercier, Louis-Sébastien. *Tableau de Paris.* Paris, 1790.

Miller, Margaret, M. and Sigmund Aarseth. *Norwegian Rosemaling.* New York: Charles Scribner's Sons, 1974.

Odom, William M. *History of Italian Furniture.* New York: The Archive Press, 1961.

Payne, Christopher. *The Price Guide to Nineteenth Century European Furniture.* Woodbridge, England: Baron Publishing, 1981.

Pellissier, Michele. *Bois et meubles peints.* Paris: Dessain et Tolra, 1976.

Percier, Charles, and Pierre Fontaine. *Recueil des décorations intérieures.* Paris, 1801, 1812.

Ritz, Josef M. *Alte bemalte Bauernmöbel.* Munich: Georg Callwey, 1938.

Rubi, Christian. *Trésors de mon pays: Mobilier peint du pays bernois.* Neuchâtel: Edition du Griffon.

————. Translated by Monique Picard. *La peinture sur bois et autres techniques ornamentales.* Lausanne: Editions de L'Aire, 1964.

Setterwall, A., et al. *The Chinese Pavilion at Drottningholm.* Malmö: Allhems Förlag, 1972.

Sheraton, Thomas. *Cabinet-Maker and Upholsterer's Drawing-Book.* 1791–94. Reprint. New York: Dover Publications, 1972.

————. *Cabinet Dictionary.* London, 1803.

Söderberg, Bengt. *Manor Houses and Royal Castles in Sweden.* Malmö: Allhems Förlag, 1975.

Thornton, Peter. *Authentic Decor: The Domestic Interior 1620–1920.* New York: Viking, 1984.

Toller, Jane. *Papier-Mâché in Great Britain and America.* Newton, Massachusetts: C.T. Branford Co., 1962.

Tomlin, Maurice. *Catalog of Adam Period Furniture.* London: Victoria and Albert Museum, 1982.

Ward, Peter Jackson. *English Furniture Designs of the 18th Century.* London: Victoria and Albert Museum, 1984.

Watin, Jean Félix. *L'Art du peintre, doreur, vernisseur.* Paris, 1773.

Watson, F. J. B. *Louis XVI Furniture.* London: Tiranti, 1960.

ACKNOWLEDGMENTS

I wish to extend my heartfelt thanks to the following people, without whose time and energies this book would not have been possible: Ruth Crocker and Marian Parry, Christie's; Phillips Hathaway and Danielle Shaw-Virtue, Sotheby's Inc.; and especially George Read at Sotheby's; Deanna Cross and Danielle Kisluk-Grosheide at the Metropolitan Museum of Art, New York; Dr. Taube Greenspan, Caramoor House Museum, Katonah, New York; Merri Ferrell, The Museums at Stonybrook, New York; Paul Schaffer, A La Vieille Russie, New York; and Marc Revillon d'Apreval, Paris.

For helping me embark on the project and making the assembling of photographs and text a far easier task than it would otherwise have been, I thank Herve Aaron, Jerry Bland, David Ferguson, François Halard, Alan J. Hartnick, Berit Henesy, the Swedish Information Service, New York; Jean-Loup Charmet, Nicolette Le Pelley of the World of Interiors, London; Evelyn Mariperisena, National Tourist Office of Spain, New York; Gustave Ortner, Cindy Sirko, Geoffrey Shakerley, Garrick Stephenson, Mish Tworkowski, and Ed Watkins.

I greatly appreciate the contribution of my cousin Dominique de Courcelles to the chapter on German painted furniture. I am also grateful to Ingrid and Monique Grenier for their help, and my assistant, Stephen Hannis, for burning the midnight oil. My deepest gratitude goes to my friends Veronique Vial and Katell le Bourhis at the Metropolitan Museum of Art, Peter Krueger at Christie's, and Christian Duvernois, all of whom were generous with their time and knowledge.

To Brigitte Demeter I owe particular thanks for the photographs of her collection.

I am indebted to the following fine interior designers whose work either illustrates the book directly or whose inspiring use of painted furniture has encouraged me in my preparation of the book: Ronald Bricke, Mario Buatta, David Anthony Easton, Anne Eisenhower, Anthony Hail, Mark Hampton, A. Michael Krieger, Robert Metzger, J. Allen Murphy, Sandra Nunnerley, Josef Pricci, Bebe Winkler, and Llana Wyman.

My special thanks go to Lauren Shakely at Rizzoli for her professionalism and dedication to this project.

F. de D.

INDEX